THE
RITZ-CARLTON
COOKBOOK

THE RITZ-CARLTON COOKBOOK

JOHN J. VYHNANEK

HARCOURT BRACE JOVANOVICH, PUBLISHERS

San Diego   New York   London

Library of Congress Cataloging in Publication Data

Vyhnanek, John J.
    The Ritz-Carlton cookbook.

    Includes index.
    1. Cookery.   2. Menus.   3. Hotels, taverns, etc.—
United States.   I. Title.
TX652.V94   1986   641.5′09744′61   86-18333
ISBN 0-15-177697-0

Editorial work by Ken Rivard, Jody Adams, Larry Rothstein, Dennis Campbell and Lyn Stallworth
Photography by Janet Knott
Design by Larry Rothstein and Dennis Campbell
Recipe testing by Jody Adams
Project development by dmc associates, inc., Boston

Printed in the United States of America
First edition
A B C D E

CONTENTS

FOREWORD

It is with great pleasure that I welcome you to *The Ritz-Carlton Cookbook*, as we celebrate the hotel's diamond anniversary.

For nearly sixty years, The Ritz-Carlton, Boston has epitomized elegance, style and sophistication. Bostonians have looked to the hotel for the standard of a refined way of life. Through our doors have come some of the most celebrated people of the twentieth century—Winston Churchill, John F. Kennedy, Charles Lindbergh, Judy Garland and Cole Porter, to name but a few.

But the most indelible memories for our guests may be the delights of the menu. The tradition of Auguste Escoffier is alive and well in our kitchen, under the vigorous command of Chef John Vyhnanek. During the last five years, Chef Vyhnanek has brought an innovative spirit to the menu without violating the principles established by Escoffier. Patrons may now select a range of food that not only includes rack of lamb and clam chowder, but also offers a spicy Sichuan bean curd and sautéed veal with prosciutto and sage.

The chefs of our sister hotels in Atlanta, Buckhead (uptown Atlanta), Laguna Niguel (California) and Naples (Florida) have made their own contributions. Through the introduction of regional American specialties and the influence of other culinary cultures, they too are helping to keep our Ritz-Carlton tradition in the forefront of modern cuisine.

In the following pages, Chef Vyhnanek explains his approach to food and cooking. I'm sure you'll find his book to be as enjoyable and thoughtful as the man I work with every day.

Sigi Bräuer, General Manager
The Ritz-Carlton, Boston

INTRODUCTION

Never has working in a kitchen been so exciting. Americans are passionately rethinking their attitudes about how and what they eat. A guest from The Ritz-Carlton of sixty years ago might walk through Back Bay today and not recognize half the food served in Boston's present restaurants. In the midst of such change, The Ritz-Carlton remains enduringly popular. With the other members of the hotel staff, I've worked diligently to keep abreast of the public's evolving tastes, while never violating the standard of excellence that has characterized the hotel since its inception.

César Ritz, the famous Swiss *hôtelier*, strove to create an atmosphere in his establishments that duplicated that of a fine private home. Such households would include a highly trained kitchen staff. Ritz allied himself with the most creative young chef of his day, Auguste Escoffier. What modern cooks tend to forget, in their rush to dispense with "heavy" French sauces, and their overreliance on grilling, is that Escoffier was the premier innovator of his own time, that much of his own work was a rebellion against the highly adorned, ornate, excessively grand cuisine of the eighteenth and early nineteenth centuries. Part of Escoffier's task was to convince his patrons that hotels were capable of producing an *haute cuisine* surpassing that of the aristocracy's own private kitchens. In good measure, he succeeded. However, today's culinary superstars are as apt to come from storefront restaurants with postage-stamp-sized kitchens as they are from luxury hotels. And unlike Escoffier's clientele, modern diners want to cook fine dishes *themselves*, in their own homes—an unthinkable proposition in the master's time.

Which brings us to this cookbook. As chef of The Ritz-Carlton, Boston, I'm the steward of several distinct traditions. One of those traditions is classical French cooking, in the style of Escoffier, which has been served in Ritz hotels around the world. Another tradition is the elegant presentation and serving of food—The Ritz-Carlton is the last hotel in the city to use silver service, that is, transporting food from kitchen to dining room on sterling trays and executing the final steps of an entrée's preparation at the diner's table. The danger in continuing such traditions is the tendency to become moribund, to allow your standards to become so rigid that they block any influence at all from the outside. On the other hand, if you abandon tradition completely then you fall prey to the worst sort of culinary one-upmanship, of joining the competition to see who can produce the weirdest, the most expensive, the trendiest food in town.

The recipes in this book result from the creative tension of maintaining a balance between those two extremes.

My own background gives me a unique perspective on this whole process. I'm the first internally promoted American to become chef of The Ritz-Carlton, Boston. But an American with an eye over his shoulder toward Europe. My upbringing had an enormous influence on how I react to food today. I come from an extended Czechoslovakian-German-American family that would rather have gone hungry than eat a meal composed of the sort of open-the-can-and-heat-it-up ingredients that were regularly featured in my friends' diets. I can remember second-grade classmates pestering me to swap my goose sandwiches for their own peanut butter and jelly. On our upstate New York farm we grew our own vegetables and raised our own chickens, ducks and geese. My father hunted deer, rabbit and pheasant. In the spring he netted shad and herring from the Hudson River. My grandfather had a smokehouse in the back yard. It was my responsibility to supply him with fresh hickory for smoking meats and fish, and when he had finished with a particular batch, to help him clean out the ashes. My mother steered me toward cooking school and my grandmother taught me how to make pastry. Some of my family's recipes have appeared on Ritz-Carlton menus and now appear in this book.

I am also part of the last group of cooks to train at the Culinary Institute of America when it was still dominated by old European masters. These chefs had risen to their positions through a continental system of apprenticeship, and their stern standards and adherence to a classical perspective have perhaps given me, and the cooks who graduated before me, a more European outlook than those who follow us. Who is to say which point of view is better?

I am, as well, someone who enjoys entertaining at home. Even as a professional, I am still delighted when my wife and I receive a compliment for a great dinner. I wanted to create a collection of recipes that would allow home cooks to present their guests, in either formal or relaxed settings, with a taste of the tradition of The Ritz-Carlton. If after reading this book and sampling the recipes, you feel that you not only have eaten well, but have understood something of the spirit of Auguste Escoffier, then I'll have succeeded.

John J. Vyhnanek, Executive Chef
The Ritz-Carlton, Boston

Some Technical Matters

In assembling the recipes for this cookbook, I inevitably encountered a conflict between my desire to include certain dishes that seemed representative of The Ritz-Carlton, and the level of technical skill I could comfortably assume in my readers. I had to strike a balance between too much discussion (which would bore accomplished cooks) and too little (which would leave many a novice floundering among the glib references to zest, clarified butter and *roux*). Early in the process I decided that the focus of this book was food, allowing the discussion of technique to creep in only when absolutely unavoidable. To simplify matters I have avoided technical terms when possible. Deglazing, for example, doesn't appear in the text of any recipe, although the actual deglazing technique is frequently described. Any bookstore with a decent cooking section carries the work of professionals whose best contribution to culinary literature is a discussion of technique and its language. Since the nature of this cookbook weights it toward recipes that often require more than a casual knowledge of the kitchen arts, I heartily encourage anyone who wants to pursue cooking seriously or seeks a deeper discussion of technique than is found here to consider the writings of Julia Child, Madeleine Kamman and Jacques Pépin, among others.

Because few people read cookbooks like novels, that is, from front to back, I thought it wise to repeat myself. If three recipes call for cleaning leeks, I don't see why readers of the second and third recipes should be burdened with flipping back through the book to the first one for instructions. On the other hand, many of the preparations will list as ingredients recipes found elsewhere in the book. Sauce recipes, for example, will often require chicken or veal stock, whose preparation is described elsewhere in the book. To have repeated the recipes for the various stocks each time one was needed would have inflated the book unnecessarily, and provided a tedious distraction for those who already have the ingredient on hand.

INGREDIENTS

An inherent part of the tradition of deluxe cooking is the use of delicious but not readily available ingredients. Even with America's expanded interest in fine cuisine, it's unlikely that truffles or fresh *foie gras* are likely to become standard items in your local supermarket, but frozen puff pastry, a great timesaver, is often available there, as are an increasing array of exotic fruits and vegetables. Almost every city now has a store specializing in luxury ingredients like dried mushrooms and handmade preserves. If an ingredient isn't immediately available, ask for it. Many shops will order an item for you. The same holds true for oriental markets. Most butchers offering high-quality meat will bone or cut to your specifications, as long as you give them a day or two of advance notice, and in the case of an unusual request will often order it for you. Where appropriate, I've suggested where an ingredient is most likely to be found.

Truffles, foie gras, smoked salmon, beluga caviar, wild mushrooms, fresh quail—these are essential elements of the style of The Ritz-Carlton. Use the highest quality ingredients you can afford. This goes for wine as well as the other ingredients. If a wine isn't good enough to drink, it isn't good enough to use in a recipe.

HERBS

Depending on the time of year and the largesse of local produce markets, a particular fresh herb may not be available. In recipes where the substitution of dried herbs for fresh is of minimal consequence I've included the dried equivalents. There are a few recipes, however, when this sort of alteration would produce an undesirable texture or color (for example, *sauce verte*). My advice in such instances is to forego the recipe until you can find the absent herb.

ACKNOWLEDGMENTS

Without the cooperation and enthusiasm of the staff and management of The Ritz-Carlton, Boston this book would never have been possible. I would like to thank Patricia Cutler, the hotel's public relations manager, for developing this project; Becky Leighton and Julia Scalzi Reynolds for the hours they spent typing my notes and recipes; Dennis Dale, executive sous-chef, and Stephen Hunn, The Cafe chef, who compiled and tested recipes from The Ritz-Carlton, Boston restaurant menus; my kitchen staff for their patience during the writing process; James Radosta, food and beverage director, and his assistant, Joseph Nova, for their expertise; Christian Russinoux, Bruno Mella, François LeCoin and Josef Lageder—the chefs of our sister hotels—for their contributions to Chapter 12; Sigi Bräuer, general manager of The Ritz-Carlton, Boston, for his willingness to excuse me from meetings; Henry Schielein, former general manager of the hotel and, at present, general manager of The Ritz-Carlton, Laguna Niguel, who helped inspire the creation of the cookbook; and Larry Rothstein, Dennis Campbell, Ken Rivard and Jody Adams, who worked tirelessly to bring the book to life.

I'd like to thank my wife, Bess, for her patience, understanding and assistance while I was writing the recipes and text. Lastly, a special thanks to my mother, Julia, who always encouraged me to become a chef.

THE
RITZ-CARLTON
COOKBOOK

CHAPTER 1

APPETIZERS

No restaurant review, no menu synopsis, no friendly recommendation produces as powerful an impression as a chef's appetizers. New patrons regard first courses with the nervous scrutiny of railroad passengers asked to admit a convict into their compartment. The encounter sets the tone for the evening. A great appetizer reassures everyone. A weak starter raises doubts ("I hope the entrée is better than this!" or "Maybe I should have ordered something simpler"), placing all the greater burden on the next course. Exactly how The Ritz-Carlton, Boston responds to that challenge is the subject of Chapter One.

When I first came to the hotel, almost a decade ago, the appetizer selection had remained essentially unaltered for more than thirty years. Culinary time, at least in the case of appetizers, had come to a stop. But I was aware the American palate had broadened considerably since the hotel opened its doors sixty years ago. My own apprenticeship in the hotel was part of America's expanding interest in good food. Even Boston, the most resolutely traditionalist of all American cities, was becoming sophisticated. As chef, one of my major responsibilities has been to select the best of the new cuisine while retaining the best of the old. Oysters, caviar, melon and prosciutto—these were the favorites of Ritz-Carlton patrons, and we've kept them on the menu. Not because they're traditional, but because they taste good.

Sometimes I've offered an American interpretation of a classic French dish. *Foie gras* is one example. American customs authorities, in their zeal to protect us from tainted meat, ban the importation of uncooked duck or goose livers. Until now, lovers of foie gras have had to survive on the canned (cooked) variety. In France, it's served uncooked, a rosy slab of pressed goose liver, seasoned with Cognac, black truffles and pepper—accompanied by a glass of crisp Alsatian gewürztraminer. The canned item doesn't compare. It seemed stupid to deny our patrons fresh foie gras simply because we couldn't import the French product. I sniffed around until I found a good American foie gras prepared in the French manner, without cooking. Purists accused me of sacrilege. But fresh is fresh and canned is canned. To quibble over country of origin rather than taste is to lose sight of the forest for the trees. Fresh duck foie gras—from the Catskills, of all places—tastes quite good, thank you. I'm proud to have added it to the menu.

Our most popular appetizer is also a recent addition: *gravlax*, a cured, unsmoked salmon. Only Norwegian salmon—flown daily to the hotel—has the tender, moist flesh requisite for this preparation. In the freezing water of Norwegian fjords, salmon grow thick insulating coats of fat (thus adding moisture to their flesh). Norwegian fisherman also wait several days after capturing the fish before killing it. Hormones that are secreted into the fish's system during its netting and that could potentially toughen the salmon's flesh are given time to dissipate.

Changing tastes have accounted for other additions to our appetizer selection. For centuries people of the Mediterranean littoral have eaten mussels. On this side of the Atlantic, mussels, as well as lobsters, were long disparaged as poor man's fare. Lobster, once regarded as cheap fare to feed Boston's Irish immigrants, found favor much sooner than did the suspicious-looking mussel, which gourmets deemed too "foreign." Fortunately, taste has prevailed over prejudice, and Ritz-Carlton patrons can now enjoy mussels steamed with white wine and saffron, a delicious introduction to any meal.

The Ritz-Carlton offers an enormous variety of appetizers. Menus for The Dining Room, The Cafe and private functions provide first courses that include items Auguste Escoffier would have recognized—smoked salmon, caviar, and oysters—as well as recent innovations that I've introduced. The following recipes encompass both the old and the new, so you can set the tone for your own dinner menu, whether traditional or more aligned with modern tastes.

Gravlax

Saumon Mariné à la Norvégienne

Serves 6

SALMON AND MARINADE

1 pound fresh Norwegian salmon fillet, skinned
1 tablespoon black peppercorns
1 tablespoon juniper berries
2 tablespoons kosher salt
1 tablespoon sugar
1 tablespoon lemon juice
2 tablespoons coarsely chopped fresh dill
1 medium onion, cut into ¼″ slices

SWEET MUSTARD SAUCE

¼ cup Dijon mustard
1 tablespoon sugar
2 tablespoons Akvavit
1 tablespoon finely chopped fresh dill
2 tablespoons water
1 tablespoon vegetable oil

GARNISH

6 leaves Bibb lettuce
6 sprigs fresh dill
6 slices pumpernickel bread, trimmed of crusts and cut in half

Place the salmon fillet in a stainless steel or Pyrex baking dish. It's important that you don't use an aluminum pan in this recipe—the marinade will interact with aluminum, causing the fish to discolor.

To make the marinade, begin by rolling a heavy saucepan over the peppercorns and juniper berries to crush them. Combine the peppercorns, juniper berries, salt, sugar, lemon juice, chopped dill and sliced onion in a non-aluminum bowl. Coat both sides of the salmon with the marinade, pouring the excess into the bottom of the dish. Cover the dish tightly and refrigerate it. Allow the salmon to marinate for 3 days, turning the fillet once each day, and taking care each time to cover the dish tightly. Marinating fish is a delicate preparation, easily overpowered by the aromas of other food in the refrigerator; pay special attention to keeping the dish sealed.

Blend all the ingredients in the mustard recipe at the same time you prepare the gravlax. The sauce will need a few days in the refrigerator to absorb the flavor of the seasonings.

When the salmon has finished curing, remove it from the dish and scrape off the marinade. Cutting on the bias, slice the fillet into paper-thin sheets. A sharp knife with a narrow, flexible blade works best.

TO SERVE: For each plate, drape 2 slices of gravlax atop a leaf of lettuce—a splash of red and green. Dab a tablespoon of mustard sauce to one side of the salmon, garnish with a sprig of fresh dill and 2 half-slices of pumpernickel bread.

Steamed Mussels with Saffron and Thyme

Moules Étuvées au Safran et Thym

Serves 4

Fresh, crusty French bread is indispensable for soaking up the rich juice in the bottom of the bowl.

¼ cup olive oil
40 mussels, washed and cleaned of their beards
3 large cloves garlic, minced
¼ cup minced shallots
6 sprigs fresh thyme
1 cup dry white wine
½ teaspoon saffron threads, crumbled
Salt and freshly ground white pepper to taste

Loaf of French bread to accompany the finished mussels

Heat the olive oil in a large saucepan over medium-high heat. Add all the remaining ingredients except salt. Cover the pan and increase the heat to high. Steam the mussels for about 5 minutes, giving the pan an occasional shake so they cook evenly. The mussels are done as soon as they open. Discard any that refuse to open—a closed shell indicates the mussel was dead before it reached your pot.

When the mussels have finished steaming, take the saucepan off the heat and remove the mussels. Arrange them in the soup bowls and cover to keep them warm while you finish the broth. Place the saucepan back on the heat and reduce the cooking liquid, now an aromatic stock, by half. Add a pinch of salt to taste and pour the liquid over the mussels.

BELUGA CAVIAR

Caviar Garni

Serves 2

I've recommended *beluga* caviar for this appetizer because that's what we serve at The Ritz-Carlton, Boston. Beluga is the name of the largest member of the sturgeon family. The large-grained roe, after salting and seasoning, become one of the world's most coveted delicacies. Connoisseurs may haggle over taste distinctions, but the other factor, besides flavor, influencing the price for caviar is the size of the grains of roe. *Ossetra* and *sevruga*, smaller sturgeon, produce smaller-grained roe. The giant glossy beads of beluga, the most expensive grade, gleam like black pearls—shining, elegant and simple. For those of you who wish to pursue the matter further, I highly recommend Jerry Stein's *Caviar! Caviar! Caviar!*, the most detailed volume I've ever seen on the subject.

2 ounces beluga caviar

GARNISH

2 tablespoons hard-boiled egg yolk, sieved
2 tablespoons hard-boiled egg white, sieved
1 small onion, diced into ¼" pieces
2 tablespoons finely chopped parsley
2 tablespoons sour cream
4 slices white bread, trimmed of crusts, toasted and cut in half

TO SERVE: Place an ounce of caviar at the top of each plate. Arrange the garnishes in a crescent around the rim of the plate, beginning with the egg yolk. Serve the toast warm from a napkin-lined tray.

RITZ-CARLTON PÂTÉ IN PUFF PASTRY

Pâté Maison en Croûte

Serves 10

This is a long recipe and a lot of work, but its spectacular presentation and wonderful taste are well worth the effort. You'll need a special *pâté en croûte* mold—available in specialty kitchenware stores. Buy the 8-cup size and make sure it has hinged sides and a removable bottom panel. The dimensions are approximately 13″ x 4″ x 3½″.

FORCEMEAT

3 pounds boneless pork shoulder or butt, untrimmed of fat
3 cloves garlic, chopped
5 shallots, sliced ⅛″ thick
1 cup Cognac
½ cup water
1 tablespoon pâté spice (also called *Épice Parisienne*, available in specialty food stores, or combine the following ingredients to make your own:
      ½ teaspoon dried thyme
      ½ teaspoon dried basil
      ¼ teaspoon dried marjoram
      ¼ teaspoon crumbled bay leaf
      ½ teaspoon ground cloves
      ½ teaspoon ground ginger
      ½ teaspoon paprika
      ½ teaspoon freshly ground white pepper
      ½ teaspoon freshly ground black pepper)

FORCEMEAT FINISHING INGREDIENTS

½ cup whole pistachio nuts, shelled and peeled
1 tablespoon chopped truffles
1 cup smoked ham, cut into ½″ cubes (about ½ pound)
2 teaspoons salt
1 teaspoon freshly ground white pepper

PUFF PASTRY CRUST

2 pounds puff pastry (available in 1-pound packages at grocery stores)
2 tablespoons unsalted butter
1 tablespoon flour
1 large egg, beaten

SAUCE

2 fresh peaches, peeled and stoned
1 tablespoon chopped ginger root
½ cup apricot preserve
¼ cup peach liqueur
¼ cup port

GARNISH

10 leaves Bibb lettuce
10 cherry tomatoes
1 bunch watercress

The preparation of the forcemeat and the assembly and baking of the pâté stretch over the length of 3 days. The puff pastry and sauce should be prepared on day 3. The pâté will be ready to serve on day 4.

PREPARING THE FORCEMEAT: Cut the pork and any attached fat into 1″ cubes. The fat *must* be included to insure a moist pâté. In a large bowl toss the cubes with the garlic, shallots, Cognac, water and pâté spice. Marinate the mixture, covered, in the refrigerator for two days, stirring it thoroughly once each day.

MAKING THE PASTRY: On the day the pâté is to be baked, roll the dough into 2 rectangles approximately ⅛″ thick. Make 1 rectangle 12″ x 20″, large enough to line the mold with ½″ overhang. Make a second rectangle 4½″ x 12½″, large enough to cover the top of the mold with ½″ overhang; this will be the cover. If you use commercial puff pastry, you'll probably have to cut and paste several sheets together to make the proper-sized rectangles. Carefully seal the seams.

Coat the mold with the 2 tablespoons of butter, dust it with flour, then fit the larger rectangle of pastry snuggly into the mold. Place the second rectangle of pastry on a baking sheet lined with parchment. Refrigerate the mold and baking sheet while you complete the forcemeat.

Using a food processor, purée the cold pork and marinade in batches until smooth, emptying the finished batches into a single large bowl. After you've puréed the entire mixture, blend in the pistachio nuts, chopped truffle, smoked ham, salt and pepper.

Test the forcemeat for seasoning by sautéing a tablespoon of the mixture. Allow it to cool before tasting. Remember that the pâté will be served cold, so the test piece should be tasted cold. Adjust the seasoning, if necessary.

Preheat oven to 350 degrees.

Remove the baking sheet and the mold from the refrigerator. Fill the mold with the forcemeat, 1 cup at a time. The mixture will be fairly firm, so press down on each batch to eliminate any air bubbles. When the mold is full, smooth the top of the forcemeat.

Brush the overhanging edges of pastry dough with beaten egg. Place the second smaller sheet of dough over the top of the mold. Squeeze the 2 sheets together at the overhanging edges and trim any areas, such as the corners, of excess dough. Roll these trimmed pieces of dough to ⅛″ and cut them into decorative shapes—sun, moon, stars, leaves. They will be attached to the top sheet of pastry. To finish the pastry, roll and crimp the overhanging edges as you would a pie crust. Cut 3 small holes in the center of the top to allow steam to escape during cooking. Brush the top with beaten egg and attach the pastry decorations, then brush the decorations as well.

Place the assembled pâté on a cookie sheet in the center of the preheated oven. Bake for 1 hour and 45 minutes or until the internal temperature of the pâté reaches 150 degrees when tested with a meat thermometer. Rotate the pâté once during baking to insure even cooking.

When the pâté has finished baking, allow it to cool at room temperature for 2 hours. *Do not try to unmold it yet! It's not completely set!* Refrigerate the pâté overnight.

To make the sauce, purée all the sauce ingredients in a food processor until smooth.

To unmold the pâté, remove the pins that hold the hinged sides of the mold together. Pry away the sides and bottom of the mold. Run a thin paring knife between the crust and the mold, if necessary.

TO SERVE: Cut the pâté into slices ½" thick. Discard the first slice—it's mostly crust. Arrange the pâté on plates with leaves of Bibb lettuce and garnish with cherry tomatoes and sprigs of watercress. Serve the sauce on the side.

SNAILS IN GARLIC BUTTER

Escargots à la Bourguignonne

Serves 4

As everyone knows, snails are simply a diversion from the true pleasure of this dish—the opportunity to soak up garlic butter with crusty slices of French bread.

24 large snails

GARLIC BUTTER

½ pound unsalted butter, softened
2 tablespoons finely chopped parsley
1 tablespoon minced garlic
1 tablespoon lemon juice
1 tablespoon cayenne pepper

French bread, sliced and toasted

Preheat oven to 425 degrees.

Blend the butter, parsley, garlic, lemon juice and cayenne pepper into a smooth paste.

Divide the snails among 4 individual oven-proof dishes. Top each snail with 2 tablespoons of garlic butter. Bake the snails until the butter melts and begins to bubble (about 15 minutes).

SHRIMP RÉMOULADE

Rémoulade aux Crevettes

Serves 6

RÉMOULADE SAUCE

1 cup mayonnaise (See recipe on page 105.)
¼ cup celery, diced into ¼″ pieces
½ cup scallions, diced into ¼″ pieces
¼ cup finely chopped parsley
¼ cup prepared horseradish, squeezed of juice
1 tablespoon lemon juice
2 tablespoons mild brown mustard (Gulden's, for example; not Dijon)
2 tablespoons ketchup
1 tablespoon Worcestershire sauce
1 tablespoon distilled white vinegar
1 clove garlic, minced
1 tablespoon hot Hungarian paprika
1 teaspoon salt
1 tablespoon sugar

SHRIMP

4 cups fish stock (recipe on page 32) or water
½ cup celery, diced into ½″ pieces
½ cup onions, diced into ½″ pieces
2 bay leaves, crumbled
4 cloves, whole
1 tablespoon cayenne pepper
36 raw large shrimp, in their shells

GARNISH

6 leaves Bibb lettuce
1 head iceberg lettuce, shredded
2 tomatoes, each cut into 6 wedges
12 lemon wedges
12 stuffed green olives
12 black olives
6 sprigs parsley

Rémoulade sauce should be made a day in advance so the various ingredients have time to work their influences on one another. Blend everything together and leave the sauce, tightly covered, in the refrigerator overnight.

The next day, combine the stock or water with the vegetables and seasonings in a large saucepan over high heat. As soon as the mixture starts to boil, reduce the heat and let it simmer for 3 minutes.

Add the shrimp and cook, uncovered, for 4 minutes.

Drain the shrimp and run them under cold water to stop the cooking. Peel and devein them, then put them in the refrigerator until well-chilled (about 1½ hours).

TO SERVE: In a medium-sized bowl combine the shrimp and the rémoulade sauce. For each serving, place a leaf of Bibb lettuce on a salad plate and mound ¼ cup of shredded lettuce in the center. Top with 6 shrimp. Garnish each plate with a few tomato and lemon wedges, both kinds of olives and a sprig of parsley.

Curried Seafood in Puff Pastry Shells

Coquilles de Fruits de Mer à la Morlesienne

Serves 4

PUFF PASTRY SHELLS

1 teaspoon butter
½ pound puff pastry (available in 1-pound packages at grocery stores)
1 large egg, beaten

SEAFOOD FILLING

1 tablespoon unsalted butter
1 tablespoon finely chopped shallots
4 raw medium shrimp, peeled and deveined
16 cape scallops
1 tablespoon Madras curry powder
1 teaspoon minced garlic
1 tablespoon finely chopped parsley
¼ pound cooked lobster meat
¼ pound Alaska king crabmeat
2 tablespoons Cognac
½ cup heavy cream
Salt and freshly ground white pepper to taste

4 sprigs parsley, for garnish
Sweet mango chutney, for garnish

Preheat oven to 375 degrees.

To make the shells, begin by greasing a baking sheet with 1 teaspoon of butter. Then roll out a ½-pound sheet of puff pastry to a thickness of ⅛″.

Cut 4 scallop-shaped shells, approximately 3″ wide, out of the sheet. Brush each shell with beaten egg and place it on the buttered baking sheet. Bake the shells for 15 minutes, or until they puff up and turn golden brown. After removing the shells, increase the oven temperature to 400 degrees.

To make the seafood filling, melt the butter in a sauté pan over medium heat. Sauté the shallots for 30 seconds and then add the shrimp, scallops, curry powder, garlic and parsley. Sauté for 1 more minute.

Add the lobster, crab and Cognac and cook for 1 minute.

Now add the heavy cream and continue cooking over high heat until the liquid coats the back of a spoon (about 1 more minute). Season the sauce with salt and pepper.

TO SERVE: Warm the scallop shells for 5 minutes in the oven. Using a sharp knife, delicately split each shell into a top and bottom half. Place the bottom halves on serving plates. Spoon the curried seafood over the pastry bottoms, then top with the remaining halves. Garnish each plate with a sprig of parsley and a tablespoon of sweet mango chutney.

OYSTERS ROCKEFELLER

Huîtres Rockefeller

Serves 4

1½ pounds raw spinach
1½ tablespoons unsalted butter
16 oysters on the half shell
¼ cup dry white wine
1 teaspoon + 1 tablespoon finely chopped shallots
Salt and freshly ground white pepper to taste
¼ cup Pernod
⅛ teaspoon freshly grated nutmeg
½ cup heavy cream
⅛ teaspoon cayenne pepper
½ cup grated Parmesan cheese
1 egg yolk, from a large egg

2 cups rock salt

Pick the stems off the spinach leaves. Grasp the stem in one hand; pinch the undersides of the leaf together with the other. Pull the stem up through the leaf. In addition to removing the stem, this technique removes the fibrous vein that runs through the leaf. Thoroughly rinse the leaves in cold running water to remove any sand or grit. Nothing will spoil a dish faster than the gritty texture of unwashed greens. Air-dry the spinach or pat it dry with paper towels.

Melt ½ tablespoon of the butter in a large, heavy-bottomed sauté pan. Sauté the spinach over high heat until the leaves wilt, releasing some of their water (about 1 minute). Drain the leaves in a colander, then chop them coarsely. Your original 1½ pounds of raw spinach should end up as 1 cup of chopped, cooked spinach.

Remove the oysters from their shells. Bring the white wine, 1 teaspoon of the chopped shallots and a pinch of salt to a boil in a large, heavy-bottomed saucepan over medium-high heat. Reduce the heat to medium-low, add the oysters and simmer for 2 minutes. Remove the oysters with a slotted spoon when their edges begin to curl and look frilly. Continue cooking the poaching liquid until it has reduced to 2 tablespoons, then remove from the heat.

Melt the remaining tablespoon of butter in a sauté pan over medium heat. Sauté the remaining tablespoon of shallots for 1 minute, then add the spinach, Pernod, salt, pepper and nutmeg. Cook for 1 more minute.

Off the heat, whisk the heavy cream, cayenne pepper, Parmesan cheese and egg yolk into the reduced poaching liquid. You should end up with a smooth paste.

Preheat the broiler.

On individual oven-proof serving dishes place 4 oyster shells in a layer of rock salt. Put a poached oyster in each shell, add a tablespoon of the spinach mixture and top with the cream and cheese paste.

Broil the oysters for 4 minutes, until they're golden and bubbling. Serve immediately.

CLAMS CASINO

Palourdes Casino au Four

Serves 4

CASINO BUTTER

½ pound unsalted butter, softened
¼ cup sweet red bell peppers, diced into ¼″ pieces
¼ cup green bell peppers, diced into ¼″ pieces
2 tablespoons lemon juice
2 tablespoons dried bread crumbs

CLAMS

32 littleneck or cherrystone clams on the half shell
32 1″ squares of raw bacon (cut from 6–8 standard bacon slices)

2 cups rock salt

4 lemon wedges, for garnish

Preheat the oven to 425 degrees.

Blend the ingredients for casino butter in a bowl or food processor. If you use a food processor, make sure to use the plastic blade—a metal blade will purée into oblivion the colorful peppers you've so painstakingly diced.

Use 4 individual oven-proof serving dishes. Layer each dish with ½ cup of rock salt, then 8 clams. Top each clam with a spoonful of casino butter and a square of bacon. Give the clams a little wiggle to be sure they're firmly embedded in the rock salt and won't tip as you move the serving dishes.

Bake the clams for 5 minutes, then pass them under the broiler to crisp the bacon. Serve bubbling hot on the oven-proof dishes with lemon wedges.

SMOKED SALMON GALETTE WITH CUCUMBER SAUCE

Galette de Saumon Fumé, Fondue de Concombres

Serves 8

1½ pounds smoked salmon, sliced paper-thin
¼ pound unsalted butter, softened
1 tablespoon finely chopped fresh dill
¼ cup heavy cream
2 cucumbers
1 tablespoon vegetable oil
Salt and freshly ground white pepper to taste
8 large spinach leaves, washed and picked of stems
½ cup sour cream
2 ounces beluga caviar

8 sprigs fresh dill, for garnish
8 lemon wedges, for garnish

Line 8 3-ounce custard cups with smoked salmon. Use 1½ ounces of salmon per cup. Refrigerate the cups after lining.

Combine 12 ounces of the smoked salmon, the butter and the fresh dill in the bowl of a food processor. Blend until the mixture is very smooth (about 3 minutes). Scrape down the side of the bowl frequently so the mixture blends evenly. With the machine running, add the heavy cream in a slow, steady stream. Turn the machine off as soon as the cream is incorporated into the mixture. Spoon the mixture into the chilled, lined custard cups—about 2½ ounces per cup. Refrigerate the galettes until firm.

To make the fondue, peel the cucumbers, cut them in half lengthwise and remove the seeds. Chop coarsely, then purée the pieces with the vegetable oil in the food processor. Season the purée with salt and pepper. Place the purée in a fine sieve over a bowl and allow it to drain for 2 hours.

TO SERVE: Line 8 salad plates with the spinach leaves. Unmold one galette atop each spinach leaf. Top with 1 tablespoon of sour cream and then top the sour cream with ¼ ounce of caviar. Place 2 tablespoons of cucumber fondue to the side of each galette. Garnish each plate with a sprig of dill and a lemon wedge.

Chapter 2

Soups and Stocks

lmost every banquet or private function at the hotel includes a soup course. I believe in soup, whether as an intermezzo between appetizer and entrée, or as a meal in itself. Few preparations rival soup's versatility of presentation or its happy ability to absorb new ingredients. The invention of vichyssoise, for example, that stately old duchess of chilled soups, owes less to culinary invention than plain and simple accident. Fortunately, the accident occurred in a Ritz-Carlton kitchen, where the chef had the genius to recognize his good luck.

Louis Diat, chef at The Ritz-Carlton, New York during the first part of this century, is credited with inventing vichyssoise. An apocryphal version of the event places him in the kitchen cooler one morning, going through the previous evening's leftovers. To his horror, a container of potato-leek soup, usually served hot, had been left uncovered. Moreover, a pitcher from an overhanging shelf had toppled on its side, spilling heavy cream into the uncovered container. Carelessness infuriated Diat. He was a man of legendary rages. When raised in anger, his voice cut over the sound of all the other activity in the kitchen. Diat saw the cream and exploded. Cooks came running to see what was wrong.

But Diat, like all great chefs, had a talent for turning disaster on its head. He stirred the cream into the cold soup and demanded some chopped chives from one of the worried cooks. He passed the cold soup among his anxious staff. Not bad, not bad at all. Someone wanted to know, what would the new soup be called? Vichyssoise, the resourceful Diat replied, after Vichy, the birthplace of his grandmother.

Feelings run high in our own Ritz-Carlton kitchen when it comes to soup. Charles Banino, executive chef during the fifties and sixties, developed the minestrone recipe described in this chapter. His *sous-chef*, Al Giannino, cut a formidable figure with a chopping knife. Al loved to dice vegetables for minestrone. Carrots, red and green peppers, onions—all manner of vegetables skipped through the silver blur of his blade, mounding in piles like perfect mosaic tiles. Al took complete responsibility for the minestrone, and for as long as he worked at The Ritz-Carlton, Boston, nobody else dared make the soup. We've named the minestrone in his memory.

Homemade soups, especially the ones associated with classic French cuisine, often intimidate amateur cooks. True, great soups usually start with great stocks, but the untutored image of how a stock is born often has more in common with Charles Dickens than with contemporary kitchen technique. People imagine an army of scullery maids chopping a week's worth of celery and onions, tossing this into a vat with a dozen chicken carcasses and a barrel of white wine, then simmering the mixture from Easter until Christmas, by which time all that's left is a dribble of ambrosia.

In fact, I use my mother's recipe for chicken stock. Until I grew up and went to cooking school I never knew that soups were supposed to be difficult. How could they be difficult if my grandparents (all four of them lived with us in a farmhouse) tossed them off so easily? In those days, the farmers of upstate New York drove around in trucks, selling vegetables off their tailgates. Supplemented by a chicken from the Vyhnanek coop, these vegetables worked their way into my family's soups. What could be simpler?

This chapter includes the basic recipes for veal, chicken and fish stocks. From these roots the mighty soup tree springs in all directions—broths, consommés, cream soups (my personal favorites) and the thick or hearty soups that verge on stew. Ritz-Carlton soups hew closely to seasonal or geographic availability. Boston's abundance of seafood, for example, allows us to produce exquisite versions of both clam and fish chowder.

A few of the following recipes represent old dishes I've rejuvenated with a modern fillip of spices or condiments. In the case of jellied madrilène, for example, a dollop of sour cream and dash of fresh beluga caviar have refreshed this grand dish. Other soups, newcomers like the cream of scallop and saffron, became successful in the The Cafe before joining the menu of The Dining Room. I firmly believe that a restaurant's willingness to develop a repertoire of fine soups speaks directly to its commitment to quality. Likewise, a good soup made at home, whether a hearty chowder for a Saturday lunch or a sinfully rich vichyssoise as an elegant prelude to rack of lamb, says that a host and hostess truly care for their guests, investing not just their money, but their time and concern as well.

RITZ-CARLTON CLAM CHOWDER

Chowder de Palourdes

Serves 8–10

Chowder is one of the great regional specialties of New England. Entire books have been devoted to chowder recipes alone: thick chowders, thin chowders, chowders using salt pork and chowders that do not, chowders with vegetables (tomatoes and corn are popular), chowders with barely a hint of cream and others as unrepentantly rich as the most luxurious French cream soups. The following two recipes are our favorites, unchanged in sixty years of service at the hotel. If you prefer thinner chowder than the ones below, simply add more clam juice, fish broth or light cream.

2 cups potatoes, diced into ½″ cubes
½ pound unsalted butter
3 tablespoons salt pork, diced into ¼″ pieces
1 cup onions, diced into ¼″ pieces
¾ cup flour
6 cups clam juice
2 pounds fresh clam meat, coarsely chopped (available at seafood
  markets)
2 cups light cream
1 cup heavy cream
Salt and freshly ground white pepper to taste

Begin by partially cooking the potatoes. Put them in a saucepan and cover them with water. Bring the water to a boil. Reduce the heat until the potatoes are just simmering. Allow them to simmer about 3 minutes; they'll still be firm. Immediately plunge them into cold water to stop the cooking, then drain and set aside.

In a large, heavy-bottomed stock pot, melt the butter. Add the salt pork and sauté over low heat until it turns light brown (5–7 minutes).

Add the onions and continue sautéing over low heat until translucent (4–5 minutes).

MAKING THE ROUX: *Roux* is a cooked combination of flour and butter that will act as the thickening agent when you add the liquid ingredients. To make the roux, add the flour to the butter, salt pork and onions. Cook the roux for 5 minutes, stirring constantly; otherwise your soup will have a floury taste. Pay attention to the heat. Burning the roux is worse than not cooking it at all, as a burned roux will give your soups a scorched flavor.

While making the roux, warm the clam juice in a saucepan.

Slowly ladle the warm clam juice into the stock pot, stirring constantly. Increase the heat to medium. Keep stirring until you've blended the roux and the clam juice completely and the mixture is thick and smooth.

Add the chopped clams and continue to cook over medium heat for 5 minutes.

Add the cream (both kinds) and potatoes. Season with salt and pepper. Reduce the heat until the chowder is just simmering. Let it simmer over low heat for 15 minutes, stirring occasionally to prevent the ingredients from sticking to the bottom of the pot.

Serve immediately.

Ritz-Carlton Fish Chowder

Chowder de Poisson

Serves 8–10

2 cups potatoes, diced into ½″ cubes
6 cups fish stock (See recipe on page 32.)
1 pound cod or haddock, cut into 1″ cubes
½ pound unsalted butter
3 tablespoons salt pork, diced into ¼″ pieces
1 cup onions, diced into ¼″ pieces
¾ cup flour
2 cups light cream
1 cup heavy cream
Salt and freshly ground white pepper to taste

Begin by partially cooking the potatoes. Put them in a saucepan and cover them with water. Bring the water to a boil. Reduce the heat until the potatoes are just simmering. Allow them to simmer about 3 minutes; they'll still be firm. Immediately plunge them into cold water to stop the cooking, then drain and set aside.

In this recipe the fish is also partially cooked before it is added to the chowder. In a large saucepan bring the fish stock to a boil. Add the fish, then reduce the heat to low. Simmer the fish for 3–4 minutes, or until barely done. Remember, it will cook more later in the recipe. Remove the fish and let it cool. Strain the fish stock, then return it to the saucepan and keep it warm over very low heat.

In a large, heavy-bottomed stock pot, melt the butter. Add the salt pork and sauté over low heat until it turns light brown (5–7 minutes).

Add the onions and continue sautéing over low heat until translucent (4–5 minutes).

MAKING THE ROUX: *Roux* is a cooked combination of flour and butter that will act as the thickening agent when you add the liquid ingredients. To make the roux, add the flour to the butter, salt pork and onions. Cook the roux for 5 minutes, stirring constantly; otherwise your soup will have a floury taste. Pay attention to the heat. Burning the roux is worse than not cooking it at all, as a burned roux will give your soups a scorched flavor.

Slowly ladle the fish stock into the stock pot, stirring constantly. Increase the heat to medium. Keep stirring until you've blended the roux and the fish stock completely and the mixture is thick and smooth.

Add the cream (both kinds) and potatoes. Season with salt and pepper. Reduce the heat until the chowder is just simmering. Let it simmer over low heat for 15 minutes, stirring occasionally to prevent the ingredients from sticking to the bottom of the pot.

Wait until 5 minutes before serving to add the fish. This prevents the fish from overcooking and crumbling into small pieces.

LOBSTER BISQUE

Bisque de Homard

Serves 6–8

1 leek
1 2-pound live lobster
2 tablespoons vegetable oil
½ cup onions, diced into ¼″ pieces
½ cup celery, diced into ¼″ pieces
½ cup carrots, diced into ¼″ pieces
2 cloves garlic, minced
2 medium tomatoes, diced into ½″ pieces
2 bay leaves, crumbled
1 tablespoon finely chopped fresh tarragon (or 1 teaspoon dried)
1 teaspoon finely chopped fresh thyme (or ½ teaspoon dried)
1 teaspoon black peppercorns
1 cup dry white wine
¼ cup Cognac
2 cups fish stock (See recipe on page 32.)
3 cups light cream
2 cups heavy cream
Salt and freshly ground white pepper to taste

PREPARING THE LEEK: Treat leeks with care or they'll ruin your dishes with an unpleasant grittiness. To prepare the leek, first cut the green part off the stalk. Then cut the leek in half lengthwise to within 1″ of the root. Fan the leaves apart as you hold the stalk under running water. Be sure to flush all the sand out. Clean the stalk and chop enough thin slices to fill ½ cup. Wrap the remainder and refrigerate it for another use.

SPLITTING A LIVE LOBSTER: Fresh lobster is essential for a great bisque, so the recipe calls for a lobster, split while still alive, then cut up and added directly to the pot. Although this may seem like an intimidating prospect, a simple procedure kills the lobster instantly—the spinal cord is severed with your first incision.

On a cutting board directly in front of you, place the lobster with its head to the right and tail to the left (reverse this if you're left-handed). Hold the tail with a towel so you don't scratch yourself on any of the spines. Hold a large knife above the lobster as though to split it lengthwise. Insert the tip of the knife into the joint between the head and tail.

Lower the knife firmly to split the lobster's head lengthwise. Now rotate the lobster so the tail is to your right. Continue holding the lobster with the towel. Although the lobster is now dead, the muscles may contract sharply, so there's still a danger of scratching yourself.

Split the tail.

Clean the lobster by removing the sand sack (the organ located right behind the eyes) and the intestine.

With a large knife, chop the lobster—head, tail and claws—crosswise into pieces 1″ thick.

In a heavy stock pot or Dutch oven, heat the oil until it starts smoking (use high heat). Add the lobster and sauté until the pieces turn a bright red. Reduce the heat to medium and add the leek, onions, celery, carrots, garlic, tomatoes, bay leaves, tarragon, thyme and peppercorns. Continue sautéing for 10 minutes.

Take the pot off the burner to add the white wine and Cognac. (You don't want to ignite yourself.) Return the pot to the burner, add the fish stock and cook for 5 minutes more. Add both kinds of cream and season with salt and pepper. Turn the heat to low and let the bisque simmer for 30 minutes.

Take the bisque off the heat and remove the lobster pieces. Set the meat aside and discard the shells.

Strain the bisque, a cup at a time, through a fine sieve. Press down on the solids to extract as much liquid as possible.

Return the bisque to the heat and add the lobster pieces 2 minutes before serving.

CHILLED POTATO AND LEEK SOUP

Potage Crème Vichyssoise

Serves 8

4 large leeks
½ cup unsalted butter
4 cups onions, sliced ¼″ thick
4 cups chicken stock (See recipe on page 31.)
4 cups potatoes, peeled and sliced ¼″ thick
3 cups light cream
Salt and freshly ground white pepper to taste

1 tablespoon fresh chives, cut into ½″ lengths, for garnish

PREPARING THE LEEKS: Treat leeks with care or they'll ruin your dishes with an unpleasant grittiness. To prepare leeks, first cut the green part off the stalks. Then cut each leek in half lengthwise to within 1″ of the root. Fan the leaves apart as you hold the stalk under running water. Be sure to flush all the sand out. Now cut the stalks into thin slices. You should end up with 4 cups.

In a large, heavy-bottomed saucepan, melt the butter over low heat, add the leeks and onions and cook slowly until they soften (about 25 minutes), stirring frequently.

Add the stock and bring it to a boil, then add the potatoes. Reduce the heat to a simmer and let the soup cook for 1 hour.

When the soup has cooked for 1 hour, take it off the heat and purée it in small batches in a food processor or blender until it's very smooth. Refrigerate the soup and chill until it's very cold. If you want to hasten the process, use an ice bath, replenishing the ice frequently.

TO SERVE: Chill soup bowls in the freezer. Using a wire whisk, beat the cream into the soup and season it with salt and pepper. If you'd like an even silkier texture, strain the soup through a cheesecloth. Serve the soup in chilled bowls and garnish with the chopped chives.

CREAM OF MUSHROOM SOUP

Potage Crème de Champignons

Serves 6

Cream soups are undoubtedly my favorites. Once you learn this basic soup recipe you can vary it in several ways. A pinch of fresh tarragon or thyme will give an interesting twist to the flavor. Purée the finished soup in a food processor if you like very smooth soups—just use extra caution when puréeing anything that's hot. I place cream of mushroom soup in a class by itself because of the different taste sensations, depending on whether you use plain, white button mushrooms, morels, or any of the wild mushrooms now commercially available. But why let your imagination stop there? The basic cream soup recipe works with just about any vegetable—asparagus, broccoli, cauliflower or tomato, to name only the standards.

3 cups chicken stock (See recipe on page 31.)
3 tablespoons unsalted butter
2 tablespoons onion, diced into ¼″ pieces
1 tablespoon minced shallots
1 pound white mushrooms, sliced ¼″ thick
2 tablespoons flour
1 cup heavy cream
Salt and freshly ground white pepper to taste

Bring the chicken stock to a boil in a saucepan over high heat. Remove it from the heat and keep the pot covered so the stock stays warm.

In a heavy-bottomed saucepan melt the butter over medium heat. Add the onions and shallots and sauté until translucent (about 3 minutes). Add the mushrooms and continue cooking for another 3 minutes. Turn the heat to low.

MAKING THE ROUX: *Roux* is a cooked combination of flour and butter that will act as the thickening agent when you add the liquid ingredients. To make the roux, add the flour to the butter, onions, shallots and mushrooms. Cook the roux for 5 minutes, stirring constantly; otherwise your soup will have a floury taste. Pay attention to the heat. Burning the roux is worse than not cooking it at all, as a burned roux will give your soups a scorched flavor.

Add the chicken stock, one ladle at a time. As you pour the stock into the pan keep stirring vigorously so the roux and stock blend completely. When you've added all the stock, bring the mixture to a simmer and allow it to bubble gently for 15 minutes. Then add the heavy cream and adjust the seasoning with salt and white pepper.

Serve immediately in warmed soup bowls.

Scallop and Saffron Bisque

Bisque de Coquilles Saint-Jacques au Safran

Serves 6–8

Begin by poaching the scallops in the fish stock. Poaching has a dual purpose—it cooks the scallops and helps give the stock flavor.

4 cups fish stock (See recipe on page 32.)
2 pounds sea scallops
4 tablespoons unsalted butter
1 cup onions, diced into ¼″ pieces
1½ cups carrots, diced into ¼″ pieces
12–15 saffron threads, crumbled
4 cups heavy cream
Salt and freshly ground white pepper to taste
¼ cup dry white wine

2 tablespoons fresh chives, cut into ½″ lengths, for garnish

To poach the scallops, bring the stock to a boil in a large pot. Add the scallops and reduce the heat until the liquid is barely simmering. Poach the scallops for 3–4 minutes, or until they're barely cooked, but still tender. Be careful not to overcook them. Off the heat, remove the scallops and rinse them immediately under cold running water to stop the cooking. When the scallops have cooled, drain and cut them into ¼″ slices and set aside until the bisque is almost finished. Reserve the stock.

In a heavy-bottomed saucepan, melt the butter over medium heat. Add the onions, carrots and saffron, cover the pan and reduce the heat to low. Let the vegetables cook for 15 minutes. Give them an occasional stir so they cook evenly.

Now add the fish stock, heavy cream, salt and pepper. Let the bisque simmer 15 minutes longer, or until the vegetables are tender.

Remove the saucepan from the heat. Purée the soup in small batches in a food processor or blender until very smooth.

TO SERVE: Warm soup bowls in the oven. While the bowls are warming, bring the wine to a boil in a sauté pan over high heat, then reduce the heat to medium and let the wine bubble for 2 minutes to burn off the alcohol. Add the sliced scallops and toss them in the wine for 1 minute, just enough to heat them through. Divide the scallops among the heated bowls, pour in the bisque and garnish the soup with chopped chives.

RITZ-CARLTON FISH STEW

Bouillabaisse à la Ritz-Carlton

Serves 6–8 as a main course

Don't be put off by the intimidating list of ingredients—bouillabaisse is not difficult to prepare if you exercise a little forethought and read the recipe thoroughly before beginning. The most difficult aspect of the preparation is the timing. You add the various kinds of seafood at different times so that nothing overcooks. Before starting out, read through the directions for splitting a live lobster on page 20.

4 medium tomatoes
2 large leeks
½ cup olive oil
1 cup onions, sliced ¼″ thick
2 tablespoons coarsely chopped fresh basil (or 1½ teaspoons dried)
10–12 saffron threads, crumbled
3 cloves garlic, minced
½ cup Pernod
6 cups fish stock (See recipe on page 32.)
Salt and freshly ground black pepper to taste
2 1-pound live lobsters
8 littleneck clams in their shells (Scrub the shells clean.)
16 mussels, washed and cleaned of their beards
8 very large shrimp, peeled and deveined
¼ pound red snapper, skin on, cut into 1″ pieces
¼ pound haddock, skin on, cut into 1″ pieces
¼ pound halibut, skin on, cut into 1″ pieces
8 medium sea scallops

GARNISH

3 tablespoons parsley or fennel leaves, coarsely chopped
1 loaf French bread
½ pound garlic butter (See recipe on page 8.)

Bring 6 cups of salted water to a boil. Drop the tomatoes into the water for 15 seconds, then plunge them into ice water to stop the cooking and shrivel the skins. When the tomatoes have cooled their skins will slide off easily. Cut the peeled tomatoes in half, crosswise, and squeeze out the seeds. Chop them coarsely into ½″ pieces, discarding the stems.

PREPARING THE LEEKS: Treat leeks with care or they'll ruin your dishes with an unpleasant grittiness. To prepare leeks, first cut the green part off the stalks. Then cut each leek in half lengthwise to within 1″ of the root. Fan the leaves apart as you hold the stalk under running water. Be sure to flush all the sand out. Now cut the stalks into thin slices. You should end up with 2 cups.

Heat the olive oil in a large Dutch oven over medium heat and sauté the leeks, onions, basil and saffron for 4 minutes. Add the tomatoes, garlic and Pernod and cook for an additional 2 minutes.

Add the fish stock, season with salt and pepper and increase the heat. Bring everything to a boil, then reduce the heat to medium and let the stock and vegetables simmer for 20 minutes.

While the stock is simmering, split the lobsters. Take out the gravel sack and intestine. Using a large knife, cut the head, tail and claws into pieces 1½″ thick.

After the stock and vegetables have cooked for 20 minutes, add the clams; cover the pot and allow them to cook for 5 minutes. Next, add the mussels, shrimp and lobster, and continue cooking, with the pot covered, for another 4 minutes.

Add the fish and scallops last, cooking them in the *uncovered* pot for 4 minutes. If there are any mussels or clams that have still not opened after this last cooking period, pick them out of the bouillabaisse and discard. They were probably dead before you started cooking them. Never take a chance with seafood that isn't utterly fresh—it could be tainted.

TO SERVE: Transfer the bouillabaisse to a soup tureen or warmed individual soup plates. Be careful not to break the pieces of fish as you lift them. Garnish the tureen or soup plates with chopped fresh fennel or parsley and serve with slices of warmed French bread brushed with garlic butter.

Minestrone Al Giannino

Soupe aux Légumes Giannino

Serves 8–10

The amount and variety of the vegetables in this recipe are up to you. What follows is Al Giannino's particular preference, but you can certainly add or substitute your own favorites. Minestrone makes a great meal when accompanied by a salad and a loaf of crusty French bread.

3 medium tomatoes
1 small leek
¼ cup ditalini (small tube-shaped pasta)
2 tablespoons olive oil
1 tablespoon salt pork, diced into ¼″ pieces
¼ cup onion, sliced ¼″ thick
¼ cup celery, diced into ¼″ pieces
¼ cup yellow turnip, diced into ¼″ pieces
¼ cup cabbage, cut into 1″ pieces
¼ cup carrots, diced into ¼″ pieces
½ cup fresh spinach leaves, washed and coarsely chopped
3 cloves garlic, minced
¼ cup fresh green beans, diced into ½″ pieces
¼ cup navy beans, soaked overnight, boiled 10 minutes, drained
¼ cup canned chickpeas, drained
½ cup frozen lima beans
1 tablespoon finely chopped fresh basil (or 1½ teaspoon dried)
2 teaspoons finely chopped fresh rosemary (or 1 teaspoon dried)
2 tablespoons tomato paste
6 cups chicken stock (See recipe on page 31.)
Salt and freshly ground black pepper to taste

1 tablespoon finely chopped parsley, for garnish
1 cup grated Parmesan cheese, for garnish

Bring 6 cups of salted water to a boil. Drop the tomatoes into the water for 15 seconds, then plunge them into ice water to stop the cooking and shrivel the skins. When the tomatoes have cooled their skins will slide off easily. Cut the peeled tomatoes in half, crosswise, and squeeze out the seeds. Chop them coarsely into ½″ pieces, discarding the stems.

PREPARING THE LEEK: Treat leeks with care or they'll ruin your dishes with an unpleasant grittiness. To prepare the leek, first cut the green part off the stalk. Then cut the leek in half lengthwise to within 1″ of the root. Fan the leaves apart as you hold the stalk under running water. Be sure to flush all the sand out. Now cut the stalk into thin slices. You should end up with ½ cup.

Bring 2 cups of salted water to a boil over high heat. Add the ditalini pasta and cook for 7–9 minutes. Tip into a colander and rinse under cold running water.

In a heavy-bottomed saucepan, heat the olive oil over low heat. Sauté the salt pork, stirring constantly. When the pork turns golden, add all the remaining ingredients except the pasta, chicken stock, salt, pepper, parsley and cheese. Cover and let cook over low heat for 10 minutes, stirring occasionally.

When 10 minutes have elapsed, add the chicken stock, season with salt and pepper and bring to a boil. Reduce the heat to a simmer. Cook the soup for 20 minutes, or until the vegetables are tender, skimming off any foam that rises to the top.

TO SERVE: Ladle the minestrone into heated soup plates and add 1 tablespoon pasta. Garnish each serving with chopped parsley. Serve Parmesan cheese on the side.

•

CLARIFIED BROTH

Consommé

Yields 3 quarts

Nothing can reduce the frustrated cook to tears quite like consommé. Alas, no book can provide an absolutely foolproof recipe for success. The steps involved in making a good consommé are deceptively simple, causing beginners to forget that what the directions lack in complexity they more than compensate for in precision. The margin for error is extremely small—a second's inattention can spoil the whole clarifying process. Yet there are specific reasons why a broth fails to become crystal clear. If your first attempt didn't work, play culinary detective with yourself: Did you stop stirring at the exact instant the stock began to boil? Did you let the consommé *slowly* simmer, or was it bubbling too fast? Were you careful not to break the "raft" on top of the soup? Did you begin with an absolutely fat-free stock?

1½ pounds extra-lean ground beef
4 egg whites, from large eggs
½ cup tomato, diced into ¼″ pieces
¼ cup carrots, diced into ¼″ pieces
½ cup onions, diced into ¼″ pieces
¼ cup celery, diced into ¼″ pieces
6 parsley stems (no leaves), finely chopped
2 teaspoons black peppercorns
1 bay leaf, crumbled
4 quarts cold, fat-free chicken or veal stock (See recipes on pages 31 and 30.)
Salt to taste

In a cool, heavy-bottomed stock pot beat the beef and egg whites with a heavy spoon until they're a frothy mass. Add the remaining ingredients and bring the pot to a boil over high heat, constantly stirring and scraping the bottom to make sure nothing sticks.

As soon as the pot begins to boil, stop stirring! Reduce the heat to low and let the pot *slowly* simmer for 1 hour. As the stock bubbles, particles of egg white harden around solid bits of vegetables, meat and other particles that would cloud the stock. The bubbling action carries the particles to the surface, where they form a solid "raft."

After the consommé has simmered for 1 hour, carefully lift off the raft of coagulated egg white. Strain the broth through 3 layers of rinsed cheesecloth and season with salt.

MAKING A TOMATO-CHICKEN CONSOMMÉ: Some recipes call for a tomato-chicken consommé (jellied madrilène, for example). You can make one by following the regular consommé recipe, substituting tomato juice for half the chicken stock.

JELLIED TOMATO CONSOMMÉ

Consommé Madrilène

Serves 6

Many people who used to dismiss jellied consommé as a hopelessly archaic dish, more appropriate to the toothless and enfeebled than to modern diners, have changed their minds after tasting it with the additional zip of sour cream and beluga caviar.

1 envelope unflavored gelatin
½ cup cold water
4 cups tomato-chicken consommé (See recipe on page 28.)
Salt and freshly ground white pepper to taste

GARNISH

6 tablespoons sour cream
1 ounce beluga caviar
6 sprigs fresh dill

Soften the gelatin in the cold water, then whisk the mixture into the tomato-chicken consommé. In a heavy-bottomed saucepan, bring the consommé to a boil over high heat, then reduce the heat to low. Season with salt and pepper and let it simmer for 15 minutes.

Pull the pan off the heat and strain the consommé through 3 layers of rinsed cheesecloth. Allow it to cool and then ladle it into individual soup cups. Refrigerate the cups until the consommé is firm (several hours).

TO SERVE: Top each cup with a tablespoon of sour cream, a dab of caviar and a sprig of fresh dill.

VEAL STOCK

Fonds de Veau

Yields about 2 quarts

3 pounds meaty veal bones, washed in cold water (Have your
   butcher cut the bones into 2″ pieces.)
½ cup onions, diced into ½″ pieces
¼ cup celery, diced into ½″ pieces
½ cup carrots, diced into ½″ pieces
1 clove garlic, whole
1 medium tomato
1 bay leaf, whole
1 teaspoon black peppercorns
1 teaspoon finely chopped fresh thyme (or ½ teaspoon dried)
Salt to taste
¼ cup water
3 quarts cold water

Preheat oven to 425 degrees.

In a roasting pan, brown the veal bones for 1 hour. Distribute the vegetables around the bones and continue to roast for another 45 minutes, or until the vegetables are well-browned. Remove the pan from the oven and transfer bones and vegetables to a heavy-bottomed stock pot.

Put the roasting pan over low heat (atop the stove) and add ¼ cup water. Using a wooden spoon, scrape the brown bits of caramelized meat juices off the surface of the pan, stirring them into the water. Take the pan off the heat and pour the juices into the stock pot.

Add all the remaining ingredients to the pot. Cover with 3 quarts of cold water. Bring the pot to a boil over high heat. Reduce the heat to low and simmer for 6 hours, skimming off the foam as it rises to the surface of the stock. All stocks require skimming as they cook. Not only are you removing elements that could detract from the stock's flavor, but as the skimming progresses the stock becomes clearer.

Remove the pot from the heat. Strain the stock through 3 layers of rinsed cheesecloth or a chinois (a conical metal strainer with very fine holes, available at cooking equipment stores). Taste the stock and season with salt, if necessary. Refrigerate or freeze the stock for future use.

CHICKEN STOCK

Fonds Blanc de Volaille

Yields about 5 cups

3 pounds meaty chicken bones
½ cup celery, chopped into ½″ pieces
½ cup onions, chopped into ½″ pieces
6 parsley stems (no leaves)
1 bay leaf, whole
2 teaspoons finely chopped fresh thyme (or 1 teaspoon dried)
1 clove garlic, whole
6 cups water
Salt to taste

Wash the chicken bones under cold running water. Place all the ingredients in a heavy-bottomed stock pot and bring to a boil over high heat. Reduce the heat to low and simmer for 1½ hours, skimming any impurities that rise to the surface.

Remove the stock pot from the heat. Strain the stock through 3 layers of rinsed cheesecloth or a chinois (a conical metal strainer with very fine holes, available at cooking equipment stores). Season with salt, if necessary. Refrigerate or freeze the stock for future use.

Fish Stock

Fonds de Poisson

Yields about 4 cups

2 pounds cod or haddock bones, chopped into 1″ pieces
4½ cups cold water
¼ cup celery, chopped into ½″ pieces
½ cup onions, chopped into ½″ pieces
2 teaspoons lemon juice
1 bay leaf, crumbled
1 tablespoon black peppercorns
2 teaspoons finely chopped fresh thyme (or 1 teaspoon dried)
Salt to taste

Wash the fish bones under cold running water. Place all the ingredients in a heavy-bottomed stock pot and bring to a boil over high heat. Reduce the heat to low and simmer for 30 minutes, skimming any impurities that rise to the surface.

Remove the stock pot from the heat. Strain the stock through 3 layers of rinsed cheesecloth or a chinois (a conical metal strainer with very fine holes, available at cooking equipment stores). Season with salt, if necessary. Refrigerate or freeze the stock for future use.

CHAPTER 3

PASTA AND RICE

During a recent trip to China I visited the Banpo Village excavations in Xi'an, not far from the site where hundreds of terra cotta warriors were unearthed several years ago. I was amazed that fragments of food found in Banpo tombs indicated the villagers had enjoyed a diet not only of rice, but pasta as well, *almost 6,000 years ago!* Italians say that while the Chinese may have invented pasta in the East, the Italians invented it in the West. They base their claim on a fresco in a fourth-century B.C. Etruscan tomb. I might add that various other theorists credit Arabs or Jews with the Western invention of pasta sometime in the fourth or fifth century A.D. No matter. Whoever invented pasta, it appears fairly certain that Venetians, contrary to popular mythology, were already eating it by the time Marco Polo made his famous journey to the land of Kublai Khan. I like to think of the Venetian trader as the first man to compare the Italian noodles with their Chinese equivalents, a rare gastronomic opportunity for his times.

Twenty years ago fresh pasta was sold in Boston only in the North End, a neighborhood of cramped Italian *grocerias*, of small butcher shops and of quaint produce markets. But even in this immigrant community only a handful of places offered fresh pasta for sale, and they were not the sort of places in which patrician Yankees tended to shop. A lover of homemade fettucine or ravioli was hard pressed to find these items on a menu outside the North End. Then, in the late seventies, came the vogue for small, household pasta machines and the public's increasing awareness that complex carbohydrates provided low-fat, filling meals. Suddenly Ritz-Carlton diners, who had never ventured beyond spaghetti or an occasional dish of lasagna, were asking for fresh noodles. When I put linguini with shrimp and vegetables on the menu of The Cafe it was the first time the hotel had featured a pasta entrée in almost a decade. These days we're as likely to offer our noodles tossed with lobster as with tomato and garlic. At present, we use both fresh and dry pasta. I've found that high-quality dry pasta works better in pasta salads than does its fresh equivalent. Fresh noodles have a tendency to become mushy when used in cold dishes.

The variety of rice dishes on our menu, like our pasta dishes, reflects the multi-cultural approach to food so popular with young restaurateurs today. As modern diners, what and how we eat is often as much the result of our craving for new experience as it is a desire to satisfy our hunger. I'm always on the alert for unusual approaches to familiar ingredients. The wild rice timbale featured in this chapter is the fortuitous product of a French recipe and a New World ingredient. It was only a matter of time before wild rice moved beyond its niche in regional American cuisine. *Khabsa*, a Middle-Eastern pilaf with braised lamb, is another instance of an unexpected treatment of ordinary ingredients. From time to time the royal family of Saudi Arabia, in parties of up to thirty people, visits The Ritz-Carlton. Members of the Fahd entourage often travel with the family's personal chef. This amiable old tyrant thinks nothing of using me as his personal vegetable chopper, barking out instructions in Arabic, which an interpreter gently translates into specific suggestions for slicing peppers or braising lamb. It became clear, several years ago, that I couldn't cook for the Saudi party without relinquishing my other obligations. To remedy the problem we simply relinquished the banquet kitchen for their chef's exclusive use. I jumped in whenever I could, helping to prepare the dozens of dishes that room service ferried to communal feasts upstairs. Members of the royal family sat crosslegged on an immaculate white sheet spread over the carpet. Khabsa is a favorite dish of Prince Turki. His chef introduced it to me and I now pass it on to you.

BUCKWHEAT NOODLES WITH SHREDDED CHICKEN

Pâtes Japonaises au Poulet Émincé

Serves 4–6

½ pound chicken breast, boneless
1 pound *soba* (Japanese buckwheat noodles, available at Oriental markets)
1 cup cucumbers, peeled, seeded and cut into julienne strips 1″ x ¼″

SAUCE
½ cup creamy peanut butter
2 tablespoons fresh ginger, finely chopped
2 teaspoons minced garlic
½ teaspoon red pepper flakes
½ cup soy sauce
½ cup sesame oil
½ cup water

6 dried red chili peppers, whole, for garnish
6 sprigs fresh chervil, for garnish

Bring 2 cups of salted water to a boil in a saucepan over high heat. Add the chicken breast, reduce the heat to medium and simmer until the breast is done (10–15 minutes). Remove the chicken from the water and allow to it cool. When the breast is cool enough to handle, cut it into julienne strips 1″ x ¼″. You should have about a cup of cooked chicken.

Bring a large pot of water to a boil. Add the soba, stirring rapidly until the water returns to a boil. Boil the soba for 7 minutes, or until it's cooked, but not mushy. Tip it into a colander and immediately rinse with cold water to stop the cooking.

Blend the peanut butter, fresh ginger, garlic, red pepper flakes, soy sauce, sesame oil and water to form a smooth sauce.

In a stainless steel mixing bowl, combine the cooked chicken, soba, cucumbers and peanut sauce, and toss well. Let the mixture marinate in the refrigerator for an hour.

TO SERVE: Divide the pasta among chilled individual bowls. Garnish each dish with a chili pepper and a sprig of chervil. Beware—this dish is quite spicy!

LOBSTER RAVIOLI WITH CHIVE SAUCE

Raviolis de Homard, Sauce Ciboulettes

Serves 4

2 cups fresh spinach
1 tablespoon sweet butter
1 tablespoon finely chopped shallots
½ pound cooked lobster meat (available at seafood markets), cut
  into ⅛" pieces
⅛ teaspoon freshly grated nutmeg
Salt and freshly ground white pepper to taste
40 wonton skins
1 large egg, beaten

CHIVE SAUCE

2 tablespoons finely chopped shallots
2 tablespoons dry white wine
1½ cups heavy cream
2 tablespoons chives, cut into ¼" pieces
Salt and freshly ground white pepper to taste

Pick the spinach leaves from the stem. Pinch the undersides of the leaf together and pull the stem up through the leaf. In addition to eliminating the stem, this technique removes the fibrous vein that runs through the leaf. Thoroughly rinse the leaves in cold running water to remove any sand or grit. Air-dry the spinach or pat it dry with paper towels. Cut it into ½" pieces.

Melt the butter in a sauté pan over medium heat, add the shallots and sauté for 1 minute. Add the lobster, spinach and nutmeg, blending them well, then season with salt and pepper. Allow the mixture to cook for 1 minute, then let it cool.

Arrange 4 wonton skins on a clean surface and brush all 4 edges with beaten egg. Place a teaspoon of the lobster mixture in the center of each wonton square. Fold the wontons in half so they form triangular raviolis. Use a fork to press down on the edges so they're well sealed. Repeat the process until you've used all the wonton skins. Don't try to make more than 4 at a time or you risk letting the wonton skins dry before you can make the raviolis.

In a saucepan over medium heat, simmer the shallots and white wine together until the wine has almost evaporated. Add the heavy cream and reduce by half. Add the fresh chives. Season with salt and pepper.

Bring a large pot of salted water to a boil, add the raviolis, stir until the water returns to a boil and cook for 4 minutes. Drain well, place them in a heated serving dish and cover with the sauce.

LOBSTER GRATIN WITH LINGUINI AND VEGETABLES

Gratin de Homard et Pâtes aux Légumes

Serves 4–6

1 cup carrots, cut into julienne strips 1″ x ¼″
¼ cup broccoli flowerets, cut into ½″ pieces
1½ pounds fresh linguini
4 cups heavy cream
2 tablespoons unsalted butter
1 shallot, minced
¼ cup zucchini, cut into julienne strips 1″ x ¼″
¼ cup mushrooms, sliced ¼″ thick
1 pound cooked lobster meat (available at seafood markets), cut into
  1″ chunks
½ cup dry sherry
Salt and freshly ground black pepper to taste
¼ cup grated Parmesan cheese

Preheat the broiler.

Bring a large pot of salted water to a boil. Add the carrots and cook 2–3 minutes. Scoop the carrots out of the water and plunge into ice water to stop the cooking. Bring the water back to a boil, add the broccoli and cook for 3–4 minutes. Scoop the broccoli out of the water and plunge into ice water to stop the cooking.

Bring the water back to a boil. Add the linguini, stirring rapidly until the water returns to a boil. Boil the linguini for 3–4 minutes, then tip it into a colander and immediately rinse with cold water to stop the cooking.

Bring the cream to a boil in a saucepan over medium heat. Allow it to reduce to 2 cups, then remove the pan from the heat and cover it so the cream stays warm.

In a large, heavy-bottomed sauté pan, melt the butter over medium heat, add the shallots and sauté until tender (about 2 minutes). Add the vegetables and cook 2–3 minutes. Add the lobster and stir until it's heated all the way through.

Remove the pan from the heat and add the sherry. Return the pan to the heat and boil off the alcohol (about 1 minute). Add the cream and bring the dish back to a boil. Season with the salt and pepper.

TO SERVE: Divide the linguini among individual casserole dishes. Top each dish with some of the lobster mixture and sprinkle with Parmesan cheese. Place the dishes under the broiler until the cheese is browned.

VEGETABLE LASAGNA

Pâtes Lazagnes aux Légumes

Serves 6

SAUCE

2 tablespoons olive oil
1 medium onion, diced into ¼″ pieces
1 clove garlic, minced
¼ teaspoon sugar
2 teaspoons finely chopped fresh oregano (or ½ teaspoon dried)
2 tablespoons finely chopped parsley
2 28-ounce cans crushed tomatoes
8 ounces tomato purée

FILLING

2 pounds ricotta cheese
2 large eggs
½ teaspoon freshly grated nutmeg
¼ cup finely chopped parsley
2 tablespoons finely chopped fresh basil (or 2 teaspoons dried)
Salt and freshly ground white pepper to taste
1 large eggplant
3 medium zucchini
3 sweet red peppers
¾ pound white mushrooms
½ cup olive oil

1 pound dry spinach lasagna noodles
3 tablespoons olive oil
1 pound mozzarella cheese, coarsely grated (about 2 cups)
1 large loaf French bread
Garlic butter (See recipe on page 8.)

MAKING THE SAUCE: In a large saucepan, heat the olive oil over medium heat. Sauté the onions and garlic in the olive oil until they are translucent (4–5 minutes). Add the sugar, herbs, tomatoes and tomato purée and stir to blend. Simmer, partially covered, for 30 minutes. Taste the sauce, season with salt and pepper. Take the pan off the heat. Keep it covered, so the sauce stays warm.

In a large mixing bowl, blend the ricotta, eggs, nutmeg, parsley and basil. Season with salt and pepper, set aside.

PREPARING THE VEGETABLES: When cooking the vegetables, bear in mind that they will receive additional cooking after incorporation into the lasagna, so the first time around try to leave them a little underdone.

Cut the eggplant crosswise into slices ⅛″ thick. Lay the slices out on a baking sheet and sprinkle with salt. Cover the eggplant with a dry cloth and let rest 1–3 hours.

Cut the zucchini lengthwise into slices ⅛″ thick. Slice the mushrooms to the same width. Seed and devein the red pepper, then trim it into strips ½″ wide.

Heat 2 tablespoons of the olive oil in a sauté pan over medium-high heat. Sauté the zucchini slices briefly (about 30 seconds per side) in hot oil—*take care not to overcook*—then remove the zucchini and drain on paper towels. Add 2 more tablespoons of olive oil to the pan and wait a minute for the new oil to heat. Add the pepper strips and cook them for 1 minute, stirring them so they don't stick. Cook until they just begin to soften, then remove the peppers and drain on paper towels. If the pan needs more oil, add another 2 tablespoons and wait for it to heat. Add the mushrooms and sauté for 1 minute, stirring constantly—again, don't overcook. Remove the mushrooms and set them aside. Wipe any excess salt or moisture off the eggplant slices. Add 2 more tablespoons of olive oil to the pan and wait for it to heat. Sauté the eggplant slices for 30 seconds on each side, then drain on paper towels.

In a large stock pot, bring 4 quarts of salted water to a boil over high heat. Add the lasagna noodles, stirring until the water returns to a boil. Cook the noodles for 9–10 minutes, or until they are cooked through, but still *al dente* (firm when you bite into one). Tip the noodles into a colander and rinse under cold water to stop the cooking. Put the noodles in a bowl and toss with 3 tablespoons of olive oil to keep them from sticking together.

ASSEMBLING THE LASAGNA: Rub an 8″ × 11″ × 2″ pan with 1 tablespoon of olive oil. Cover the bottom of the pan with a thin layer of sauce (about ½ cup). Layer strips of pasta over the sauce so they cover the bottom of the pan and overlap each other by ¼″. Spread all the zucchini and pepper in a single layer, then cover with a layer of pasta. Spread a third of the remaining sauce over the pasta; then cover it with the ricotta cheese mixture. Sprinkle half the mozzarella over the ricotta, then cover the cheeses with a layer of pasta. Spread half of the remaining sauce over the pasta. Distribute the eggplant and mushroom slices in an even layer, then cover with the remaining pasta. Spread the remaining sauce over the pasta and sprinkle with the rest of the mozzarella.

At this point, you can refrigerate the lasagna to cook at a later date, or you can cook it immediately. If you choose to refrigerate the lasagna, take it out 1 hour beforehand so it warms to room temperature before you begin cooking it.

Preheat oven to 350 degrees.

COOKING THE LASAGNA: Bake the lasagna for 1 hour. Slice a loaf of crusty bread (I prefer French, rather than Italian) and drizzle melted garlic butter into the cracks. Wrap the loaf in foil and put it in the oven 20 minutes before the lasagna is done. The lasagna is finished when the top is lightly browned and you can insert a knife easily. Let the lasagna repose for 15 minutes before serving. Serve with the hot garlic bread.

Spaetzle

Serves 4

4 large eggs
½ cup milk
2–2¼ cups flour
1 teaspoon salt
¼ teaspoon freshly grated nutmeg
2 tablespoons finely chopped parsley
⅛ teaspoon freshly ground white pepper
1 tablespoon vegetable oil
2 tablespoons unsalted butter

Beat the eggs in a mixing bowl until they're thoroughly blended. Add the milk and blend well. Add the flour, salt, nutmeg, 1 tablespoon parsley, pepper and vegetable oil and beat until you've worked the ingredients into a smooth dough. Begin by adding 2 cups of the flour, adding more if necessary. The dough should be moist, but not runny.

In a large stock pot bring 4 quarts of salted water to a boil. Place one-third of the dough in a colander. Using the back of a spoon, force the dough through the colander holes into the boiling water. Hold the colander at 8″–10″ above the water so the dough still in the colander doesn't cook.

The spaetzle take only 1–2 minutes to cook. They're done as soon as they rise to the surface of the water. Remove them with a slotted spoon or skimmer and spread them out on a cloth napkin or tea towel to cool. (Don't use a paper towel—the spaetzle will stick.) Repeat with the rest of the dough.

Melt the butter in a large non-stick pan over medium-high heat. Add the spaetzle and sauté until they're lightly golden, tossing them frequently so they don't stick and burn.

TO SERVE: Place the spaetzle in a warm serving dish. Garnish with the remaining tablespoon of chopped parsley. Serve immediately.

Risi Bisi

Serves 4–6

2½ cups chicken stock (See recipe on page 31.)
1 tablespoon unsalted butter
½ cup mushrooms, sliced ¼″ thick
¼ cup onions, diced into ¼″ pieces
1 teaspoon minced garlic
½ cup cooked ham, cut into julienne strips 1″ x ¼″ (about ¼
    pound)
1 bay leaf, whole
1½ cups converted rice
Salt and freshly ground white pepper to taste
½ cup cooked green peas
2 tablespoons pimentos, diced into ¼″ pieces

Bring the chicken stock to a boil in a saucepan. Remove the pan from the heat and cover it so the stock stays warm.

In a heavy-bottomed saucepan, melt the butter over medium heat. Add the mushrooms, onions and garlic. Sauté them until they soften (8–10 minutes).

Stir in the ham, bay leaf and rice. Continue cooking, stirring often, for 5 minutes.

Add the stock, season with salt and pepper, and increase the heat to high. As soon as the pan comes to a boil, reduce the heat to low, cover, and simmer for 20 minutes, without lifting the lid.

Remove the pan from the heat and let it stand, covered, for 10 minutes before serving.

TO SERVE: Remove the bay leaf, then stir the peas and pimentos into the rice. Serve risi bisi in a warmed serving dish.

SAUDI RICE PILAF

Riz Pilaf Prince Turki

Serves 6

1 medium tomato
2 cups chicken stock (See recipe on page 31.)
6 loin lamb chops, ½″ thick, trimmed of fat
Salt and freshly ground white pepper to taste
2 tablespoons vegetable oil
½ cup onions, diced into ½″ pieces
1 cup green peppers, diced into 1″ pieces
1½ cups converted rice
6 dried lemons, optional (available at specialty food stores)
2 cinnamon sticks, whole
1 cup eggplant, skin on, diced into 1″ pieces

Bring 4 cups of salted water to a boil. Drop the tomato into the water for 15 seconds, then plunge it into ice water to stop the cooking and shrivel the skin. When the tomato has cooled, its skin will slide off easily. Cut the peeled tomato in half, crosswise, and squeeze out the seeds. Chop it coarsely into ¾″ pieces, discarding the stem.

Bring the chicken stock to a boil in a saucepan. Remove the pan from the heat and cover it so the stock stays warm.

Season the lamb chops with salt and pepper.

Heat the oil over medium heat in a large Dutch oven. Brown the lamb chops on both sides in the hot oil. Add the onions and green peppers and continue cooking for 5 minutes.

Add all the remaining ingredients except the stock. Stir the vegetables so they're evenly distributed through the rice, then add the stock. Season with salt and pepper, then bring to a boil. Cover the Dutch oven, reduce the heat to low and let the pot simmer for 40 minutes, without lifting the lid. Remove the pot from the heat and let stand for 10 minutes, covered.

TO SERVE: Remove the cinnamon sticks. On an oval serving platter, arrange the chops in an overlapping row atop a mound of rice and vegetables.

WILD RICE FLAN

Timbale de Riz Sauvage

Serves 8

WILD RICE

2½ cups chicken stock (See recipe on page 31.)
1 tablespoon unsalted butter
1 tablespoon onions, diced into ¼″ pieces
1 cup wild rice
Salt to taste

CUSTARD

1 tablespoon unsalted butter
4 large eggs, beaten
⅛ teaspoon freshly grated nutmeg
1½ cups light cream
Salt and freshly ground white pepper to taste

MAKING THE WILD RICE: Bring the chicken stock to a boil in a saucepan. Remove the pan from the heat and cover it so the stock stays warm. Next, melt the butter in a heavy-bottomed saucepan over medium heat. Add the onions and sauté until they're translucent (2–3 minutes). Add the rice, stirring until the grains are completely coated with butter. Add the heated chicken stock, bring it to a boil and season it with salt. Cover the pan, reduce the heat to its lowest point and let the rice and stock cook for 40 minutes, without lifting the lid.

Remove the pan from the heat and let it stand, covered, for 15 minutes. Uncover and let cool. Drain off any remaining liquid.

MAKING THE CUSTARD AND COOKING THE FLAN: Preheat oven to 325 degrees. Coat the inside of a 1½-quart soufflé dish with the butter. In a mixing bowl, beat the eggs, nutmeg and light cream until well blended. Season with salt and pepper. Spoon the wild rice into the dish, then add the egg mixture. Bake for 40–45 minutes, or until the flan sets. Serve hot, directly from the soufflé dish.

Creole-Style Rice Pilaf

Riz Pilaf Créole

Serves 6

1 medium tomato
2 cups chicken stock (See recipe on page 31.)
2 tablespoons vegetable oil
½ cup onions, diced into ¼″ pieces
½ cup celery, diced into ¼″ pieces
½ cup green peppers, diced into ¼″ pieces
½ cup sweet red peppers, diced into ¼″ pieces
1 teaspoon minced garlic
1½ cups converted rice
2 teaspoons gumbo filé (Cajun seasoning made from sassafras leaves
    and available at specialty food stores)
1 teaspoon finely chopped fresh thyme (or ½ teaspoon dried)
1 bay leaf, whole
⅛ teaspoon cayenne pepper
Salt to taste

Bring 4 cups of salted water to a boil. Drop the tomato into the water for 15 seconds, then plunge it into ice water to stop the cooking and shrivel the skin. When the tomato has cooled, its skin will slide off easily. Cut the peeled tomato in half, crosswise, and squeeze out the seeds. Chop it coarsely into ½″ pieces, discarding the stem.

Bring the chicken stock to a boil in a saucepan. Remove the pan from the heat and cover it so the stock stays warm.

In a heavy-bottomed saucepan, heat the oil over medium heat. Sauté the onions, celery, peppers and garlic until tender (3–4 minutes). Add the rice and all the remaining ingredients, except the stock, stirring until the rice and vegetables are evenly mixed. Then add the stock and bring the mixture to a boil. Season with salt. Cover the pan, reduce the heat to low and let the pan simmer for 20 minutes, without lifting the lid.

Remove the pan from the heat and let stand, covered, for 15 minutes before serving.

PAELLA

Serves 8

1 medium tomato
4 cups chicken stock (See recipe on page 31.)
1 cup clam juice
½ teaspoon saffron threads, crumbled
⅓ cup olive oil
1 3-pound chicken, cut into 8 pieces
Salt and freshly ground black pepper to taste
1 cup onions, diced into ¼″ pieces
¼ pound chorizo sausage, sliced ½″ thick
½ cup green peppers, diced into ½″ pieces
2 cups converted rice
1 tablespoon minced garlic
½ cup pimentos, coarsely chopped
½ cup green olives, pitted
¾ cup cooked chickpeas
16 littleneck clams in their shells, scrubbed
16 mussels in their shells, scrubbed and cleaned of their beards
½ pound large shrimp, peeled and deveined

Bring 4 cups of salted water to a boil. Drop the tomato into the water for 15 seconds, then plunge it into ice water to stop the cooking and shrivel the skin. When the tomato has cooled, its skin will slide off easily. Cut the peeled tomato in half, crosswise, and squeeze out the seeds. Chop it coarsely into ½″ pieces, discarding the stem.

Combine the chicken stock, clam juice and saffron in a saucepan and bring them to a boil. Remove the pan from the heat and cover it so the contents stay warm.

Heat the olive oil in an oven-proof paella pan or wok (or a large Dutch oven, if you don't have either of these) over medium heat. Season the chicken with salt and pepper. Fry the chicken pieces (both sides) in the hot oil until they're golden and about three-quarters done (about 20 minutes). Remove the chicken from the pan.

Add the onions to the pan and sauté until tender (3–4 minutes). Add the chorizo and peppers, and cook an additional 2 minutes. Add the rice and garlic—be sure to stir everything so the rice is thoroughly coated with oil.

Add the chopped tomato, pimentos, green olives and chickpeas, stirring until all the vegetables are evenly distributed through the rice. Season with salt and pepper.

Preheat the oven to 350 degrees.

Return the chicken to the pan, add the stock and clams, then cover. Simmer for 5 minutes. Add the mussels and simmer an additional 5 minutes. Bake, covered, in the oven for 15 minutes.

Remove the cover, add the shrimp and bake *uncovered* for another 10 minutes.

Take the pan out of the oven and discard any clams or mussels that haven't opened.

To serve: Serve the paella directly from the paella pan or divide it individually among large shallow bowls. Make sure everyone receives a portion of chicken and each type of shellfish. Provide additional plates to hold the discarded shells and bones.

Ritz-Carlton Risotto

Risotto à la Ritz-Carlton

Serves 4

1 cup milk
1 cup chicken stock (See recipe on page 31.)
1 tablespoon unsalted butter
1 cup converted rice
½ teaspoon saffron threads, crumbled
Salt and freshly ground white pepper to taste
½ cup grated Parmesan cheese
1½ cups light cream

2 tablespoons finely chopped parsley, for garnish

Combine the milk and chicken stock in a saucepan and bring to a boil. Remove the pan from the heat and cover it, so the enriched stock stays warm.

In a heavy-bottomed saucepan, melt the butter over medium heat. Add the rice and coat it with the butter. Add the saffron and enriched stock and increase the heat to high. Season with salt and pepper. As soon as the mixture begins to boil, reduce the heat to low. Cover the pan and let simmer for 20 minutes, without lifting the lid.

Remove the cover, add the cheese and cream. Simmer for another 10 minutes, stirring occasionally.

To serve: Spoon the risotto into a heated bowl. Sprinkle with chopped parsley immediately before serving.

BELUGA CAVIAR
page 5

GRAVLAX
pages 3–4

PÂTÉ IN PUFF PASTRY
pages 6–8

CHILLED POTATO AND LEEK SOUP (VICHYSSOISE)
page 21

VEGETABLE LASAGNA
pages 38–39

RISI BISI
page 41

CHAPTER 4

SEAFOOD

A quick glance down the menu of The Ritz-Carlton Dining Room immediately reveals New England's strong suit—fish cookery. Halibut, lemon sole, lobster, scallops (sea scallops and the smaller Cape variety), swordfish and that most Yankee fish of all, scrod, are a few of the seafood entrées. Clams, mussels and oysters, cooked and raw, alone or in chowders, make their sundry appearances in appetizers or soups. The only Dining Room entrée soup —bouillabaisse—is a Mediterranean seafood preparation utilizing New England ingredients.

As the menu of The Dining Room changes twice each year, before I add a new entrée I ask myself, "Will someone be able to supply me with these ingredients four months from now? Will the quality remain consistently high?" Of all the items featured as main courses, local seafood is the most reliable. The availability of other exotic fish notwithstanding (thanks to air freight), we place absolute trust in our local seafood suppliers. Ideally, fish should be stored at a few degrees above freezing. As water turns to ice, the water molecules trapped inside the fish's flesh rupture the cell walls, giving the flesh a mushy texture. Many restaurants never consider that saltwater fish freeze at a lower temperature than freshwater species—twenty-eight degrees instead of thirty-two. We have a special seafood refrigerator with two compartments, each set at a different temperature. That way we can keep all our seafood as cold as possible, without freezing it.

I have my own prejudices when it comes to seafood. Norwegian salmon is one of them. Sea scallops are another. In recent years, fashionable restaurants have almost completely supplanted the meaty Atlantic sea scallop with its smaller, slightly tenderer incarnation from Cape Cod, a move that makes about as much sense to me as indiscriminately substituting filet mignon for prime rib. Each has its time and place. In years past, unscrupulous wholesalers of seafood have given sea scallops a bad name, duping the unwary purchaser with "punch-outs": scallop-shaped pieces cut out with a punch from skate or cod. But genuine sea scallops have a hearty brininess that stands out in sturdy dishes like scallop pot pie or chowder, and they have the added advantage of being a little more forgiving when it comes to cooking time. An extra thirty seconds in the sauté pan is unlikely to ruin a dozen sea scallops, but a similar oversight with Cape scallops renders them fit only for cat food.

Another of my prejudices has to do with trout. My father, a repository of fishing and hunting lore, insisted that trout, brown or speckled, merited a good deal more respect than other fish. Herring or shad mindlessly swam into his net in such copious numbers that he annually pickled five or six fifty-gallon drums of each. But a trout was an individual, a canny adversary whose incomparable taste was somehow connected with its cunning elusiveness. The Ritz-Carlton kitchen currently lacks a reliable source for great trout. To my taste the standard Idaho rainbow trout has an insipid flavor and a mushy texture, qualities I associate with its factory-style production. Sunrise fishing expeditions with my father have forever convinced me that trout bred in a stream, feeding on a diet of insects and freshwater plankton, taste far better than the fish from giant trout farms, restricted to a diet of processed liver. At present, I'm experimenting with fresh Icelandic trout delivered by plane. I'm also working with a young fish farmer in western Massachusetts who's testing the effect of various diets on the flavor of farmed native trout.

Years ago, as an indication of the dignity my father accorded the trout, he bought me an expensive Garcia fishing rod and reel, which I still use during those now infrequent opportunities for fishing. I hope there's an angler or two who will read this chapter and apply our recipe to their own early morning catches.

LOBSTER IN WHISKEY SAUCE

Homard à la Ritz-Carlton au Whiskey

Serves 4

8 tablespoons unsalted butter
2 tablespoons finely chopped shallots
1½ pounds cooked lobster meat (available at seafood markets), cut
    into 1″ pieces
½ cup bourbon
2 cups heavy cream
Salt and freshly ground white pepper to taste
1 tablespoon fresh chives, cut into 1″ lengths

Melt 4 tablespoons of the butter in a sauté pan over medium-high heat. Add the shallots and sauté 1 minute. Add the lobster meat and sauté for 1 minute.

Remove the pan from the heat and add the bourbon (never add alcohol while the pan is still over a flame—you might ignite the alcohol, and yourself).

Return the pan to the heat and cook until the whiskey has reduced by half, then remove the lobster pieces and set them aside.

Add the heavy cream to the pan and bring it to a boil. Reduce the heat to medium and let the cream simmer until it has also reduced by half, then turn the heat to low.

Cut the remaining butter into tablespoon-sized pieces. Swirl the butter into the sauce, one tablespoon at a time, always waiting until the previous tablespoon has melted before adding the next one. *Do not allow the sauce to boil—if it reaches the boiling point, it will break; that is, separate.*

Return the lobster to the pan. Toss it in the sauce until all the pieces are heated thoroughly. Season the sauce with salt and pepper.

Serve on warmed plates. Sprinkle each serving with chives.

DOVER SOLE

Soles de Douvres Sautées à la Meunière

Serves 2

In my opinion, Dover sole is the finest fresh fish in the world. Don't confuse it with the various types of flatfish called "sole" in America. Dover sole is native to European waters only, and while lemon sole, flounder and grey sole all have their particular qualities, in taste none of them quite compares to fresh English Dover sole. The following recipe requires you to cook the sole whole and fillet it afterwards. The firm white meat and large bones of Dover sole make this a particularly good fish on which to practice your boning technique.

1 stick unsalted butter
2 whole Dover soles, skinned, bone in, approximately 18 ounces
   each
1 cup flour, for dredging
Salt and freshly ground white pepper to taste
6 tablespoons salted butter
Juice from 1 whole lemon
2 tablespoons parsley, coarsely chopped

2 lemons, sliced ¼″ thick, for garnish
2 sprigs parsley, for garnish

Preheat the oven to 400 degrees.

Clarify the unsalted butter by melting it in a small pan over low heat. Skim the froth of casein that rises to the surface, then spoon out the clear yellow liquid (clarified butter) without disturbing the layer of whey in the bottom of the pan. You should end up with ⅓ cup of clarified butter. Refrigerate any extra for another use.

If the soles still have heads and tails, you may remove them now or wait until the fish is cooked. If you decide to remove them now, cut off the head just behind the gills. Dredge the sole in flour and shake off any excess. Heat the clarified butter over medium-high heat in large heavy-bottomed sauté pans, preferably oval, to near the smoking point. The size of Dover sole almost always dictates that you use a separate pan for each fish, so preparing this recipe for more than 2 requires either professional expertise, many helpers or superhuman dexterity. Carefully lower the fish into the hot butter. Season with salt and pepper. If the butter doesn't sizzle when you add the fish, the pan's not hot enough. Sauté the sole until the tail end appears to be cooked and the underside is golden brown (about 3 minutes), then *carefully* turn the fish on its other side and add 1 tablespoon of salted butter to each pan. Immediately place the pans in the oven.

Allow the fish to finish cooking in the oven (about 5 minutes). The sole is done when the flesh begins to pull away from the spine at the head end.

Transfer the fish to a heated platter. Allow it to repose for 5 minutes so the flesh has a chance to become firm before you start boning.

Remove the head and tail if you haven't already done so. Remove the fin bones that run along the outer edges of the fish. They should pull away easily. Orient the fish so the head end faces you. Run a knife down the center of the fish—over the spine—from head to tail. This cut splits the 2 top fillets. Bone the right fillet first. Using a chef's knife, carefully insert the edge of the blade under the edge of the fillet closest to the spine. Push out toward the side of the fish, separating the ribs from the fillet. Do not cut into the fish. The fillet should separate easily.

Repeat on the left side and transfer the 2 top fillets to a warmed platter.

Starting at the head end, carefully lift the comb-like spine and rib cage away from the bottom fillets. Pull the spine gently toward you. It should come away in one piece. Split the bottom fillets and check for any bones you might have missed. Transfer the bottom fillets to the platter with the top fillets. Repeat with the second fish.

To make the sauce, empty 1 of the pans of any remaining butter and return the pan to medium-high heat. Add the remaining 4 tablespoons of salted butter. As soon as the butter foams, add the lemon juice and chopped parsley. Season the sauce with salt and pepper.

TO SERVE: Line the lower edge of the platter with a row of overlapping lemon slices and garnish one end of the platter with parlsey sprigs. Pour the sauce over the fillets and serve immediately.

SAUTÉED SHRIMP WITH HOT CHILIES AND SCALLIONS

Crevettes Sautées à la Chinoise

Serves 4

Stephen Hunn, the chef of The Cafe, developed this recipe to take full advantage of the fresh shrimp we fly in from Florida daily. It reminds me of a real tongue-scorcher I once tasted at the Cleveland Restaurant in Hong Kong.

1 tablespoon sesame oil
3 tablespoons peanut oil
2 pounds large Gulf shrimp, peeled and deveined
2 dried hot chili peppers, seeds removed, cut into julienne strips
   about 2″ long
¼ cup scallions, white part only, cut into ¼″ pieces
1 teaspoon minced ginger
2 tablespoons dry sherry
¾ cup hoisin sauce (available at Oriental markets)
2 tablespoons oyster sauce
¼ cup scallions, green part only, sliced on the diagonal into ¼″
   pieces

If you assemble your ingredients in advance, this recipe takes about 4 minutes to prepare. It requires you to use a very hot pan, adding the ingredients in rapid succession and stirring constantly so nothing sticks to the hot metal surface. To facilitate the cooking, you might want to have all your ingredients lined up in small cups, ready to go, before the actual cooking starts.

In a wok or large sauté pan, heat the sesame oil and 1 tablespoon of peanut oil over high heat until they begin to smoke.

Add the shrimp and cook for 1 minute, stirring constantly.

Add the chilies and cook for 1 minute, stirring constantly.

Remove the shrimp and chilies from the wok and set them aside.

Add the remaining 2 tablespoons of peanut oil to the wok. When it starts to smoke, add the white scallions and the ginger. Stir for 15 seconds and then add the sherry.

Add the hoisin and oyster sauce. When the sauce begins to boil, return the shrimp and chilies to the pan. Cook for 1 more minute.

Serve immediately, sprinkling each portion with green scallions.

LEMON SOLE WITH BANANAS AND ALMONDS

Filets de Soles Caprice

Serves 4

1½ sticks unsalted butter
4 whole lemon sole fillets, skinned, approximately 7 ounces each
1 cup flour, for dredging
3 large eggs
3 tablespoons unsalted butter
1 large banana, sliced ¼" thick
½ cup toasted sliced almonds
¼ cup dry white wine
2 tablespoons finely chopped parsley
Salt and freshly ground white pepper to taste

4 lemon wedges, for garnish

Clarify the butter by melting it in a small pan over low heat. Skim the froth of casein that rises to the surface, then spoon out the clear yellow liquid (clarified butter) without disturbing the layer of whey in the bottom of the pan. You should end up with ½ cup of clarified butter. Refrigerate any extra for another use.

Dredge the fillets in flour and shake off any excess. Beat the eggs well. Heat the clarified butter in 2 large, heavy-bottomed sauté pans over medium heat. Dip the floured fillets in the egg wash and carefully place them in the heated butter, skin-side up. (I know—I told you to get *skinless* fillets. Fillets have 2 sides—one flat, one round; the round side is the skin-side, whether the skin is on or not.) If the butter doesn't sizzle when you add the fish, the pan's not hot enough.

Sauté the fillets until the underside is golden brown, then *carefully* turn them over and continue cooking until the skin-side is also golden. The flesh of the cooked fillets should be firm but tender, with barely any resilience. Take the pans off the heat. Place the fillets on a heated serving platter and cover to keep them warm.

To make the sauce, select one of the sauté pans, empty it of any remaining clarified butter and return it to the heat. Cut the whole butter into tablespoon-sized pieces and add them to the pan along with the bananas and almonds. Shake the pan until the butter melts and begins to foam. Do not let it get any hotter or the butter will brown.

Add the white wine and parsley and cook for 1 minute. The alcohol will evaporate and the butter and wine will bind the bananas and almonds into a sauce.

TO SERVE: Spoon the the sauce over the fillets and garnish with the lemon wedges.

GRILLED SALMON WITH CRACKED PEPPER AND BACON

Darne de Saumon Grillée aux Poivres et Lard Fumé

Serves 4

1 stick unsalted butter
2 tablespoons whole black peppercorns
4 salmon steaks, approximately 8 ounces each
Salt to taste
4 slices bacon, cut on the bias into ¼" pieces

4 lemon wedges, for garnish

Preheat the broiler.

Clarify the butter by melting it in a small pan over low heat. Skim the froth of casein that rises to the surface, then spoon out the clear yellow liquid (clarified butter) without disturbing the layer of whey in the bottom of the pan. Save ¼ cup of clarified butter for the salmon. Refrigerate any extra for another use.

Rock a heavy saucepan over the peppercorns to crack them. Brush the salmon steaks with clarified butter. Season with salt and sprinkle them with the cracked pepper. Broil under medium-high heat until half done (about 4 minutes). Sprinkle bacon over each steak and continue cooking until the salmon flesh flakes easily from the center bone (about 4 more minutes).

TO SERVE: Remove the central bone (actually part of the spine) and the large bones in the tail of the steak. Catch an edge of the skin with a fork and peel it off. Serve with lemon wedges.

SAUTÉED TROUT WITH LIME, CAPERS AND TOMATOES

Truites Sautées aux Citron Vert, Câpres et Tomates

Serves 4

2 medium tomatoes
¼ cup capers
2 whole limes
¾ cup dry white wine
8 fresh trout fillets, 3–4 ounces each
1 cup flour, for dredging
Salt and freshly ground black pepper to taste
4 tablespoons safflower oil
3 tablespoons unsalted butter, cut into thirds, softened

Bring 6 cups of salted water to a boil. Drop the tomatoes into the water for 15 seconds, then plunge them into ice water to stop the cooking and shrivel the skins. When the tomatoes have cooled their skins will slide off easily. Cut the peeled tomatoes in half, crosswise, and squeeze out the seeds. Chop them coarsely into ½″ pieces, discarding the stems. Place the chopped tomatoes in a bowl with the capers.

This recipe calls for lime zest, the colored outer rind of the fruit. The easiest way of preparing it is to use a zesting tool, a small peeler made expressly for scraping the skin off citrus fruit. A good kitchen supply house will be able to provide you with one. Failing that, you can use a peeler. Try to cut wide swatches of skin, taking care to leave the white, pithy part of the rind attached to the fruit. Scrape all the pith off the zest or the sauce will taste bitter. Strip both limes of their zest. Use a paring knife to slice it into narrow julienne strips ¹⁄₁₆″ wide, approximately 1″ long.

Place the zest in a glass with a ¼ cup of white wine to keep it from drying out while you complete the recipe. Before adding the zest to the sauce, drain it and discard the white wine.

Remove the pith from the limes to expose the sections. Use a paring knife to cut between the membranes and remove each section whole. Place the lime sections in the bowl with the tomatoes and capers.

Dredge the trout fillets in the flour, shaking off any excess. Season the floured trout with salt and pepper.

In each of 2 large heavy-bottomed sauté pans heat 2 tablespoons of safflower oil over medium-high heat. Place the trout carefully in the pan and sauté for 3 minutes on each side, or until they're golden. They should present a small amount of resistance to your touch.

Remove the pans from the heat. Put the fillets on a serving platter and cover so they stay warm.

Use only one of the pans to make the sauce. Return it to medium-high heat. Add the chopped tomatoes, capers, lime sections and lime zest (remember, throw away the marinating wine). Cook for 15 seconds, stirring carefully so you don't break the lime sections. Add the remaining ½ cup of white wine and cook for 1 more minute.

Remove the pan from the heat. Swirl the butter into the sauce, 1 tablespoon at a time, always waiting until the previous tablespoon has melted before adding the next one. Season the sauce with salt and pepper and pour it over the fish.

BROILED SCALLOPS IN A JULIENNE VEGETABLE NEST

Coquilles Saint-Jacques Grillées

Serves 4

The Ritz-Carlton, Boston now serves a number of dishes low in calories, cholesterol and salt. This is a delicious example.

1 large red bell pepper
1 large green pepper
1 large carrot
1 medium rutabaga (or 2 small turnips)
1 large summer squash
1 large zucchini
1½ pounds bay scallops
2 cups finely ground dry bread crumbs
¼ cup safflower oil

4 lemon wedges, for garnish

Cut the ends off the peppers. Remove the membrane and seeds, slice into julienne strips ⅛″ x 3″. Peel the carrot and rutabaga and cut them into julienne strips of the same size. Trim the ends off the squash and zucchini, remove the seeds and follow the same procedure.

Steam all the vegetables together until tender (about 2 minutes).

Toss the scallops in bread crumbs and shake off any excess.

Place the scallops on a broiling pan in a single layer. Sprinkle with the oil. Broil until browned (4-5 minutes) but still tender.

TO SERVE: Form a nest of steamed vegetables on each plate. Spoon the scallops into the center. Garnish with lemon wedges.

BROILED BOSTON SCROD

Cabillaud Grillé

Serves 6

What, exactly, is *scrod?* In one dictionary I saw it was listed as young cod or haddock. A *haddock?* Not in Boston! Our fish purveyors define scrod as baby cod under 2½ pounds. Baby cod has a delicate taste very different from the flavor of the adult fish (memorialized nationwide in high school cafeterias as frozen cod cakes). Perhaps the mildness of scrod accounts for its popularity—scrod has always been, hands down, the most frequently ordered entrée on all the hotel's lunch menus.

1 stick unsalted butter
6 baby cod fillets, skin on, approximately 10 ounces
3 cups dry bread crumbs, finely ground

6 lemon wedges, for garnish
6 sprigs parsley, for garnish

Preheat the broiler.

Clarify the butter by melting it in a small pan over low heat. Skim the froth of casein that rises to the surface, then spoon out the clear yellow liquid (clarified butter) without disturbing the layer of whey in the bottom of the pan. Save ¼ cup of clarified butter for this recipe. Refrigerate any extra for future use.

Roll the fillets in bread crumbs and shake off the excess.

Drizzle the fillets with butter.

Broil the fillets for 8–10 minutes, 4″ from the broiler flame, until the flesh flakes but is still moist.

Garnish with the lemon and parsley.

SWORDFISH WITH MUSTARD CREAM AND JALAPEÑOS

Espadon à la Crème Moutarde et les Poivres Mexicains

Serves 6

1¼ sticks unsalted butter
2 cups white wine fish sauce (See recipe on page 98.)
3 tablespoons Pommery mustard
6 swordfish steaks, approximately 9 ounces each
6 fresh jalapeño peppers
Salt and freshly ground white pepper to taste

Preheat the broiler.

Clarify the butter by melting it in a small pan over low heat. Skim the froth of casein that rises to the surface, then spoon out the clear yellow liquid (clarified butter) without disturbing the layer of whey in the bottom of the pan. You should end up with ½ cup of clarified butter. Refrigerate any extra for another use.

In a saucepan over low heat, warm the white wine sauce. *Don't let the sauce boil or it will separate.* Whisk the mustard into the sauce. When the sauce is hot, pull the pan off the heat and keep it covered so the sauce stays warm.

Brush the swordfish and the peppers with clarified butter. Season with salt and pepper. Grill the steaks and peppers over a hot flame or under the broiler. Turn the peppers several times. The swordfish is done when it's firm to the touch, with just a small amount of resilience. The peppers are finished when their skins have blackened.

TO SERVE: Make 3 or 4 lengthwise cuts in each of the blackened peppers, fanning the slivers out from the stem. Place a pepper fan atop each swordfish steak, slightly off to one side. Ladle the mustard sauce over the other side of the steak.

SCALLOP POT PIE

Coquilles Saint-Jacques en Cocotte

Serves 6

12 large mushrooms
1 large carrot
3 large or 4 small Idaho potatoes
2 teaspoons salt
8 tablespoons unsalted butter
2 pounds sea scallops
Salt and freshly ground white pepper to taste
2½ cups white wine fish sauce (See recipe on page 98.)
3 large leeks
1 cup fresh bread crumbs (no crust)
1 cup Ritz cracker crumbs

Cut the mushrooms into quarters. Peel the carrot and cut it into julienne pieces 1″ x ¼″. (This should make about 1 cup of julienned carrots.) Peel the potatoes and use a 1″ melon baller (an easily available kitchen tool, resembling a miniature ice cream scoop) to scoop out 24 balls, roughly 6 balls per potato.

Place the potato balls in a saucepan with 3 quarts of cold water. Bring the pan to a boil over high heat. Let the potatoes boil until they're just slightly undercooked (about 3–4 minutes).

Take the pan off the heat. Scoop the potatoes out of the water (don't throw away the water in the saucepan). Rinse the potatoes immediately under cold water to stop the cooking. Set the potatoes aside. Bring the pan back to a boil and add 2 teaspoons of salt.

Add the carrot pieces and cook until they're slightly underdone (about 2 minutes). Follow the same procedure with the carrots as with the potatoes—rinse and set them aside. When they are done, drain and pat the carrots and potatoes dry. Set them aside.

Melt 4 tablespoons of the butter in a large sauté pan over medium-high heat. Add the mushrooms and sauté 2 minutes. Turn off the heat, add the scallops and season with salt and pepper. Toss the scallops in the warm pan until they whiten on the outside, but are still raw inside (about 1 minute). Add the white wine fish sauce, potatoes and carrots; mix well and set aside.

PREPARING THE LEEKS: Treat leeks with care or they'll ruin your dishes with an unpleasant grittiness. To prepare leeks, first cut the green part off the stalks, then cut each leek in half lengthwise to within 1″ of the root. Fan the leaves apart as you hold the stalk under running water. Be sure to flush all the sand out. Follow this procedure with all 3 leeks. Drain off excess water and dice into ¼″ cubes. You should end up with 2 cups.

Preheat oven to 375 degrees if using a single large casserole dish or 425 degrees if using individual dishes.

Melt the remaining butter in a large sauté pan over medium-high heat. Add the leeks and sauté until they soften (3–4 minutes). Season with salt and pepper. Add the bread and cracker crumbs, stirring until they're completely coated with butter, then take the pan off the heat.

Either spoon the scallop-vegetable-sauce mixture into a large 2-quart casserole dish or divide it among 6 individual 2-cup casseroles. Top the casserole(s) with the sautéed leeks and crumb mixture.

Bake the individual casserole dishes until the crumb topping turns brown and the sauce is bubbling (about 15 minutes). If you use a large casserole dish, the scallops will take longer and should bake at a lower temperature so they don't dry out. If the sauce starts to bubble before the topping has browned, you can place the casserole(s) under the broiler for 1 or 2 minutes before serving.

FRESH CRAB WITH LINGUINI, TOMATO-BASIL VINAIGRETTE

Crabes aux Pâtes, Vinaigrette de Tomates et Basilic

Serves 6

VINAIGRETTE

6 medium tomatoes
1 cup safflower oil
½ cup red wine vinegar
4 tablespoons fresh basil leaves, coarsely chopped
3 garlic cloves, minced
Salt and freshly ground black pepper to taste

SALAD

24 asparagus spears
1 pound dry linguini
1½ pounds fresh crabmeat
15 sprigs watercress, picked of stems
1 medium red onion, sliced paper-thin

6 lemon wedges, for garnish

Bring 12 cups of salted water to a boil. Drop the tomatoes into the water for 15 seconds, then plunge them into ice water to stop the cooking and shrivel the skins. When the tomatoes have cooled their skins will slide off easily. Cut the peeled tomatoes in half, crosswise, and squeeze out the seeds. Chop them coarsely into $\frac{1}{2}''$ pieces, discarding the stems.

To make the vinaigrette whisk together the safflower oil, red wine vinegar, basil, garlic and tomatoes in a large bowl. Season with salt and freshly ground black pepper.

There are several schools of thought on how to prepare asparagus. The traditional method is to bend the stalk gently from tip to stem until it breaks naturally. The stem end is usually tough and fibrous and may be discarded. Another alternative is to peel deeply (take it down $\frac{1}{16}''$ all the way around) the stem end of the stalk. This eliminates much of the outer fibrous layer and provides a longer portion of edible stalk. Whichever method you use, you can peel the entire stalk if you prefer. For appearance's sake, cut all the stalks to the same length.

In a sauté pan large enough to hold the asparagus in one layer (use 2 pans, if necessary, or cook the asparagus in batches), bring $2''$ of salted water to a boil. It's essential to boil the asparagus spears in a shallow pan so they can't bang around and break apart. Blanch the asparagus in a single layer for 3 minutes, or until they're crisp but cooked. Plunge them immediately into ice water to stop the cooking, then set aside.

Bring a large pot of salted water to a boil. Add the linguini, stirring rapidly until the water returns to a boil. Boil the linguini for 9 minutes, then tip it into a colander and immediately rinse under cold water to stop the cooking.

Combine the linguini, crabmeat and watercress in a large bowl. Toss with the vinaigrette.

TO SERVE: Divide the crab and linguini salad among 6 plates. Arrange paper-thin slices of onion around the top of each plate, 2 asparagus spears on each side (pointing down), and a lemon wedge on the bottom.

Poached Salmon with Hollandaise Sauce

Filets de Saumon Pochés, Sauce Hollandaise

Serves 4

4 cups fish stock (See recipe on page 32.)
4 salmon fillets, approximately 7 ounces each
Salt and freshly ground white pepper to taste
¼ cup onions, cut into julienne strips, 2″ x ⅛″
¼ cup celery, peeled, cut into julienne strips, 2″ x ⅛″
¼ cup carrots, peeled, cut into julienne strips, 2″ x ⅛″
1½ cups hollandaise sauce (See recipe on page 101.)

4 sprigs dill, for garnish

Heat the fish stock in a saucepan until it begins to boil. Remove the pan from the heat and cover to keep the stock warm.

Season the salmon with salt and pepper. Arrange the fillets in a single layer in a large heavy-bottomed sauté pan with sides at least 2″ high. Use an additional sauté pan if necessary. Arrange the vegetables over the fillets. They must be sliced very thin or they won't finish cooking at the same time as the fish. Add the stock—it should cover the salmon by at least ½″. If 4 cups of stock aren't sufficient, add more stock or water.

Turn the heat to medium-high and bring the stock to a boil. As soon as it starts to boil, immediately reduce the heat to low so the pan is just barely simmering. Allow the fish to poach for 7–9 minutes, or until the salmon is firm, but not dry.

TO SERVE: Transfer the fillets and vegetables to a warmed serving platter. Garnish the platter with sprigs of fresh dill and accompany with a sauce boat of hollandaise.

CHAPTER 5

POULTRY

No item on the menu of The Ritz-Carlton, Boston has caused me as much grief as chicken pot pie. Our version of this New England favorite dates back to Paul Massé, the hotel's first chef. Each Saturday since the opening of the hotel, every menu, from room service to The Dining Room, has featured chicken pot pie as the daily special. Undoubtedly Mr. Massé was trying to give the dish a leg up on the ladder of sophistication when he specified canned Belgian baby carrots and pearl onions in the recipe. Had he only known how those ingredients would haunt his successor half a century later!

When I became executive chef I made it a priority to rework the recipe collection of The Ritz-Carlton, substituting fresh ingredients for canned whenever feasible. Aha! Canned carrots, even canned *Belgian baby carrots* would be swept away. Canned pearl onions—out the door! I trusted the innate good taste of our patrons to notice the difference and expected the complimentary letters to begin rolling in.

Of course, the opposite happened. Within a week of serving the new pot pie I received close to a hundred complaints, each and every one asking what had happened to the *canned* vegetables. Not without some grumbling on the part of our patrons, I stuck to my guns. The recipe included in this chapter calls for fresh ingredients. If you have a particular affection for the baby-food texture of canned ingredients, by all means go ahead and make the substitutions, but don't say I didn't warn you.

In the summer of 1984 a heat wave swept over Boston. I tried substituting cooler, lighter dishes for the Saturday special—you guessed it—chicken pot pie. Again, complaints jammed my mailbox. I gave up. Chicken pot pie is obviously a Ritz-Carlton favorite, and this chef, for one, will tamper with it no more.

One area where I've had more success is with our roast goose. I'm always astounded when I meet people who've never tasted goose. "It's all dark meat," they protest, and look at me as if I've just invited them to eat a plate of monkey. (Ducks are also entirely composed of dark meat, but why quibble with illogic?) Goose is a rich, succulent fowl, easily the equal of lamb in its meaty satisfactions. At Christmas, I include roast goose with braised cabbage on the menu of The Dining Room. This Czech dish always brings back memories of the holiday season, my large family ringing the dining room table, everyone joking as my grandfather assumed the dignified demeanor befitting the carver of such a splendid beast.

We feature duck in two different forms: roasted, as most Americans with a fondness for the crispy duckling skin familiarly know it; and sautéed, a practice that dates back hundreds of years in France, but has only recently become popular in American restaurants.

Home cooks' major concerns regarding fowl are *doneness* ("Should there be any pink coloring in the meat?") and *fat* ("Duck and goose are just too greasy for me to cook in my kitchen"). The fat problem is minimized by trimming excess fat from the bird before cooking, then as the duck or goose roasts, using an oven baster to remove the fat draining into the roasting dish. An even simpler technique is to sauté duck breasts trimmed of all fat and skin, reserving the skin for use as cracklings in the garnish.

Until ten years ago, most Americans ate their fowl well done. A suggestion of pink, even in chicken breasts, stopped forks in mid-flight to mouths. But as Americans have embraced European food, they've learned to appreciate fowl cooked medium, or even rare. At The Ritz-Carlton, we roast all types of fowl until the juices run clear yellow. But with the giant boneless breasts from French *mulard* ducks, we sauté them for only a few minutes on each side, so the meat is a rich, rosy color, equivalent to that of a medium-rare steak. Personally, I prefer fowl slightly undercooked, but not rare. Duck and goose, unlike beef or lamb, can be very chewy when cooked rare, and the happiest compromise seems to be a spot somewhere between pink and rose.

Chicken Pot Pie à la Ritz-Carlton

Poulet en Cocotte

Serves 6

POACHING THE CHICKEN

1 3-pound chicken, whole
1 cup onions, diced into ½″ pieces
1 cup celery, diced into ½″ pieces
1 bay leaf, whole
1 tablespoon black peppercorns
Salt to taste

POT PIE

6 large mushroom caps
2 slices bacon
2 large potatoes
12 pearl onions, peeled
12 baby carrots, peeled
½ cup green peas
5 tablespoons unsalted butter
1 pound puff pastry (available in 1-pound packages at grocery
   stores)
3 cups chicken stock (from poaching the chicken)
½ cup light cream
Salt and freshly ground white pepper to taste
3 cups cooked chicken meat (from poaching the chicken)
1 large egg, beaten

POACHING THE CHICKEN: Wash the chicken under cold running water. Check the cavity for the neck, giblets, heart and liver. If present, remove and save all of them, except the liver, which you can discard or save for use in another recipe.

Place the chicken and all of the poaching ingredients, including the neck, giblets and heart, in a heavy-bottomed stock pot. Add enough water to just cover the chicken—about 6 cups. Bring the water to a boil, then reduce the heat to medium-low and simmer for 1 hour and 15 minutes, or until the chicken is tender. Skim off any scum or foam that rises to the surface of the stock during cooking.

Remove the chicken from the pot and allow it to cool. Pour the cooking liquid through a fine strainer into a clean saucepan. Discard the vegetables, bay leaf, peppercorns, neck, giblets and heart. Lightly boil the stock over medium-high heat until it has reduced to 3 cups. Again, skim any impurities that rise to the surface during cooking. You will use this reduced stock to make the sauce.

When the chicken has cooled, remove all the meat from the bones. Discard the skin and carcass. Cut the meat into pieces, 2″ by ½″, and save them.

PREPARING THE VEGETABLES: Cut the mushrooms in half. Slice the bacon crosswise into ½″ pieces (you should get about 12).

Peel the potatoes. Use a 1″ melon baller (a sort of mini-scoop available in kitchen specialty stores) to cut 12 balls out of the potatoes (6 per potato). Place the balls in a saucepan with 2 quarts of cold water. Bring the water to a boil, cook the potato balls for 3–4 minutes, leaving them slightly undercooked. Remove the saucepan from the heat and scoop the potatoes out of the water. Plunge them into ice water to stop the cooking.

Return the saucepan to high heat, add 2 teaspoons of salt and bring the water back to a boil. Add the onions. Cook until tender (2–3 minutes for frozen; 4–5 for fresh). Take the saucepan off the heat, remove the onions and plunge them into ice water.

Put the pan back on the heat, bring the water back to a boil (don't add any more salt) and follow the same procedure with the carrots (3–4 minutes, leaving them slightly undercooked), first blanching them, then plunging them into the ice water.

Repeat the procedure for *fresh* peas; with frozen ones, simply defrost them and set aside until it's time to add them to the pie.

Bring the saucepan back to a boil. Add the bacon and cook for 1 minute. Drain the bacon in a colander. (You can discard the water in the saucepan now.) Plunge the bacon into the ice bath with the vegetables. After the bacon has cooled, drain the ice bath. Pat the vegetables and bacon dry and set aside until time to assemble the pie.

Melt a tablespoon of butter in a sauté pan over medium-high heat. Add the mushrooms and sauté, stirring so they don't stick, until they are tender (3–4 minutes), then set them aside.

MAKING THE CRUST: Roll the puff pastry into a sheet measuring 8¾″ x 11¾″, and ⅛″ thick. If you're using packaged dough you'll have to join two sheets together. Be sure the seam is well sealed. The pastry sheet should be large enough to cover the 8″ x 11″ baking dish you will use for the pie, leaving ¾″ of overlap on all sides. Refrigerate the dough on a baking sheet lined with parchment (a paper bag will do in a pinch) until you're ready to cover the pie.

Preheat oven to 350 degrees.

Warm the reduced chicken stock in a stock pot over medium heat.

Melt the remaining 4 tablespoons of butter in a saucepan over medium heat. Add the flour to make a roux and cook for 1 minute. Slowly add the stock, one ladle at a time, whisking vigorously until thick and well-blended. Add the light cream and season with salt and pepper. Reduce the heat to low and let simmer for 5 minutes. The sauce should be thick, but if you prefer a thinner sauce, add more cream.

MAKING THE PIE: Put the vegetables, bacon and cooked chicken in an 8″ x 11″ oven-proof baking dish. Add the sauce and blend until everything is evenly mixed. Top the baking dish with the pastry sheet and crimp the edges as you would a pie shell. Cut 4 1″ slits into the pastry sheet, to allow steam to vent during baking. Brush with beaten egg and bake for 50 minutes, or until the crust is golden and the filling is bubbling.

ROAST DUCKLING WITH POMMERY MUSTARD SAUCE

Caneton Rôti, Sauce Moutarde

Serves 4

1 5½-pound duckling, whole
Salt and freshly ground white pepper to taste
3 cups veal stock (See recipe on page 30.)
½ cup heavy cream
¼ cup Pommery mustard

To prepare the duck for roasting, remove any excess skin or fat at the openings of the neck and tail cavities. Clip the wings at the first joint (closest to the body). Season the cavity with salt and pepper.

To truss the duck, place it breast-up atop a 4′ length of butcher's twine. The tail cavity should be facing toward you. The twine should be running under the front third of the duck, emerging in equal lengths from 2 spots just forward of the wings. Lift and cross the 2 lengths of twine as though you were going to wrap a package: one string should pin the right wing against the duck's body, cross the breast diagonally and knot itself around the left leg; the other piece of twine should pin the left wing against the body, cross the breast and secure itself to the right leg. Tie the drumsticks and the tail together in a tight little bundle, closing the tail cavity. Snip off any excess twine.

Preheat oven to 400 degrees.

Prick the skin of the duck all over with a sharp roasting fork, especially around the fatty thigh area. The holes allow the melted subcutaneous fat to escape during roasting.

Place the duck on its side on a rack in a roasting pan with high sides. Roast for 1½ hours. After the first 30 minutes of roasting, turn the duck on its other side. After the second 30 minutes, turn the duck breast-up and complete the roasting. Test the bird for doneness by pricking it with a metal skewer at the thigh joint. It's done when the juices run clear yellow, not pink.

While the duck is roasting, bring the veal stock to a boil in a saucepan over medium-high heat. Lower the heat to medium and cook until the stock has reduced by half.

Remove the duck from the oven and allow it to repose for 15 minutes before carving. Cover it loosely with foil to keep it warm.

Discard the fat from the roasting pan. Set the pan over medium high heat. Add the reduced veal stock. Use a rubber spatula to loosen the caramelized particles of duck juice stuck to the pan. When all the particles have dissolved, remove the stock from the pan and strain.

Preheat the broiler.

MAKING THE SAUCE: While the duck is reposing you can make the sauce. Bring the cream and reduced veal stock to a boil in a saucepan over medium-high heat. Lower the heat so the mixture doesn't boil over, but is still bubbling rapidly. Cook until it reduces to 1 cup. Stir in the mustard, turn the heat to low and simmer for 5 minutes. Season the sauce with salt and pepper.

TO SERVE: Untruss the duck and remove the breasts, thighs and legs with the skin intact. Cut the breasts in half. Arrange all the pieces skin-side up on an oven-proof serving platter. Pass the platter under the broiler for a few minutes to crisp the skin. Serve with the mustard sauce on the side.

DUCKLING BRAISED IN RED WINE

Salmis de Caneton Bordelaise

Serves 4

4 cups veal stock (See recipe on page 30.)
1 5½-pound duckling, cut into 8 pieces (2 boneless breasts, cut in
   half, crosswise; 2 thighs and 2 legs)
Salt and freshly ground white pepper to taste
4 tablespoons flour
2 tablespoons vegetable oil
½ cup carrots, diced into ½″ pieces
½ cup onions, diced into ½″ pieces
1 tablespoon minced garlic
2 teaspoons finely chopped fresh thyme (or 1 teaspoon dried)
2 bay leaves, whole
1 tablespoon black peppercorns
3 cups dry red wine
16 pearl onions, fresh or frozen
2 teaspoons unsalted butter
16 small mushroom caps
1 tablespoon finely chopped parsley

Bring the veal stock to a boil in a saucepan over medium-high heat. Reduce the heat to medium and cook until the stock has reduced by half.

Season the pieces of duckling with salt and pepper and dredge in the flour, shaking off any excess. In a Dutch oven, heat the oil over medium-high heat until it begins to smoke. Add all the pieces of duck, skin-side down. Fry the pieces until they're crisp on both sides (about 10 minutes a side). Transfer the duck to a warmed platter and set aside. Empty the Dutch oven of all but 1 tablespoon of duck fat. (Don't throw the fat away. A tablespoon of duck or goose fat is a wonderful flavoring for braised or sautéed vegetables, or for soup.)

Return the Dutch oven to medium heat. Add the diced carrots and onions and the garlic, thyme, bay leaves and peppercorns; sauté for 4 minutes. Take the Dutch oven off the heat and add the red wine.

Return the Dutch oven to the heat and cook for 10 minutes, then add the reduced veal stock. Increase the heat to high, bring everything to a boil and add the browned duck. Reduce the heat to medium and simmer for 45 minutes, uncovered. Transfer the duck to an oven-proof serving dish and keep hot.

Reduce the sauce to 1 cup. Skim off the fat that rises to the top, then take the Dutch oven off the heat. Strain the sauce and keep it warm in a small saucepan.

If you're using fresh pearl onions, bring a pot of salted water to a boil, add the onions and cook for 2–3 minutes, or until they're tender. Rinse them under cold water to stop the cooking. If you're using frozen onions, simply defrost them.

Melt the butter in a sauté pan over medium-high heat. Sauté the mushroom caps and pearl onions until golden brown.

TO SERVE: Pour the sauce over the hot duck on the serving platter. Top the duck with the mushroom caps and pearl onions, then sprinkle with chopped parsley.

Medallions of Chicken with Pecans and Maple Bourbon Butter

Rosettes de Poulet Sautées aux Noisettes et Whiskey

Serves 4

1 stick unsalted butter
2 cups chicken stock (See recipe on page 31.)
4 large half-breasts of chicken, boned and skinned, approximately 8
    ounces each
Salt and freshly ground white pepper to taste
2 cups finely chopped pecans
1 cup + 2 tablespoons bourbon whiskey
2 tablespoons maple syrup
¼ teaspoon finely chopped fresh herb mixture (rosemary, thyme,
    sage, tarragon)
8 tablespoons unsalted butter, cut into 8 pieces, softened

Clarify the stick of butter by melting it in a small pan over low heat. Skim off the froth of casein that rises to the surface, then spoon out the clear yellow liquid (clarified butter) without disturbing the layer of whey in the bottom of the pan. Reserve ¼ cup of the clarified butter. Refrigerate any extra for future use.

Bring the chicken stock to a boil in a saucepan over medium-high heat. Lower the heat to medium and cook until you've reduced the stock by half. Set aside.

Cut each breast in half across the grain. Place each piece, called a *rosette*, between 2 sheets of plastic wrap, skin-side (the round side) down. Pound the chicken with a heavy-bottomed saucepan or flat meat tenderizer to even out the thickness of the rosettes and break down some of the muscle fibers. Each piece of meat will enlarge slightly with pounding. All should have a uniform thickness of ¼″. Season with salt and pepper. Press each rosette into the pecans until it is coated.

Heat half the clarified butter in a large, heavy-bottomed sauté pan over medium heat. Sauté half the rosettes until they brown on one side (3–4 minutes) and then turn them. Be careful not to burn the pecans or they'll turn bitter. The finished rosettes should be tender, offering a slight resistance to the touch. Transfer them to a serving platter and keep warm.

Empty the sauté pan of the cooking fat and any remaining pecans. Add the remaining clarified butter and sauté the rest of the rosettes. When they're done, place them with the first batch.

Empty the fat out of the sauté pan, but leave any pecans. Add the bourbon before returning the pan to the heat. Return the pan to high heat, slightly tilting the pan away from you in case the bourbon flames. Don't worry if it doesn't flame. Your objective is to remove the alcohol, and whether it happens by flaming or boiling doesn't matter. After the alcohol has either burned or boiled off, add the stock and reduce by one-third. Add the syrup and herbs. Lower the heat to its lowest point.

Whisk the 8 pieces of butter into the sauce, 1 tablespoon at a time, always waiting until the previous tablespoon has melted before adding the next one.

TO SERVE: Place the rosettes on a heated platter and cover with sauce.

BREAST OF MULARD DUCKLING WITH ARMAGNAC SAUCE

Magrets de Caneton Sautés à l'Armagnac

Serves 4

Magrets or *maigrets* are very large duck breasts. They come from the *mulard,* a cross between the Muscovy and Peking duck. The term *magret* comes from the French verb *maigrir,* meaning to grow thin or waste away, a reference to dietary restrictions that prevailed in ancient France during Lent. These duck "steaks," even when trimmed of fat, taste quite rich to the modern palate. Not so to the old French, accustomed to a much more generous portion of fat with their duck.

4 slices white bread
2 tablespoons unsalted butter
2 mulard duck breasts, boned, skin on, approximately 12 ounces
    each
2 cups veal stock (See recipe on page 30.)
Salt and freshly ground white pepper to taste
2 tablespoons finely chopped shallots
1 cup dry red wine
1 cup Armagnac

Cut each slice of bread into the image of a duck. Melt the butter in a sauté pan over medium heat, add the duck cut-outs and sauté on both sides until they're golden. Drain them on paper towels.

Carefully remove the skin from the magrets. In most places it can be separated by hand, except for the skin attached to the meat at a spot in the center of the breast. Use a knife to detach the skin here, but take care not to cut into the duck breast. Cut the skin into julienne strips 3″ by ⅛″.

Fry the pieces of duck skin like bacon, using a heavy-bottomed sauté pan over medium heat. They should be crisp and golden brown. Drain the pieces on paper towels, to rid them of excess fat. Don't cover them or they'll become soggy. Remove the pan from the heat and pour out the duck fat. Save 1½ tablespoons to use later in the recipe. Discard the rest or save it for flavoring soup or braised vegetables.

Bring the veal stock to a boil in a saucepan over medium-high heat. Lower the heat to medium and cook until you've reduced the stock by half. Set aside.

Season the magrets with salt and pepper. In a sauté pan over medium-high heat, heat 1 tablespoon of the duck fat. When it's hot, add the duck breasts and sauté for 3 minutes on each side (they should be medium-rare). Transfer the breasts to a cutting board so they can repose for 10 minutes while you make the sauce.

Add or subtract duck fat from the pan—you will need 2 teaspoons in the sauté pan for the next step. Heat the fat over medium-high heat. Add the shallots and sauté until they become translucent (about 1 minute). Remove the pan from the heat and add the red wine and Armagnac.

Return the pan to medium-high heat and reduce the liquid to ½ cup. Add the veal stock and reduce until there's 1 cup of sauce in the sauté pan. Season with salt and pepper.

TO SERVE: Preheat oven to 400 degrees. Put the cracklings on a baking sheet and crisp them in the oven for 5 minutes. Carve the magrets into thin slices, cutting on the bias. Fan the slices on a warmed serving platter, drizzle with the reduced sauce and sprinkle with the duck cracklings. Arrange the toasts on the edge of the platter.

CHICKEN CURRY PERCY SULLIVAN

Cari de Volaille Percy Sullivan

Percy Sullivan, the famed restaurateur from Hyderabad, India, has served a variety of condiments with this curry at The Ritz-Carlton, Boston, any or all of which you might like to accompany this dish—sweet mango chutney, pickled papaya, lime pickles (all are available at Indian or Oriental markets), finely chopped onions mixed with sour cream and sliced bananas cooked in a sugar and lemon syrup.

5 cups veal stock (See recipe on page 30.)
1 3½ pound chicken, cut into 8 pieces (2 wings, tips removed; 2
   breasts, 2 thighs and 2 legs)
2 tablespoons flour
Salt and freshly ground white pepper to taste
1 cup + 2 tablespoons vegetable oil
2 cups finely chopped onions
6 cloves garlic, coarsely chopped
½ cup coarsely chopped fresh ginger
½ cup Madras curry powder
2 tablespoons Spanish paprika
½ cup tomato purée
Salt to taste
1 teaspoon cayenne pepper
1 cup light cream
1 teaspoon finely chopped fresh parsley

Bring the veal stock to a boil in a saucepan over medium-high heat. Lower the heat to medium and cook until you've reduced the stock by half. Set aside.

Rinse the chicken under cold water and pat dry. Dust each of the pieces with flour and season with salt and pepper. In a Dutch oven over medium-high heat, heat 2 tablespoons of the oil until it begins to smoke. Fry the chicken on each side until the skin is crisp and golden (10–12 minutes per side). Remove the chicken, drain on paper towels and set aside.

Add the remaining cup of oil to the Dutch oven and heat over medium-high heat until it starts to smoke. Add the onions and fry until golden, stirring constantly. Add the garlic and ginger and fry for 1 minute, stirring constantly. Remove the Dutch oven from the heat and pour off the oil, keeping the onions in the pot.

Return the Dutch oven to medium-high heat and add the curry powder, paprika, tomato purée and reduced veal stock. Cook for 5 minutes, then remove from heat. Purée the mixture in small batches in a food processor. Return the puréed mixture to the Dutch oven with the chicken, salt and cayenne pepper. Bring to a boil, then lower the heat and simmer for 30 minutes. Add the cream and cook for 5 minutes more.

TO SERVE: Transfer the chicken to a warmed serving platter. Cover the chicken with the sauce, sprinkle with the chopped parsley.

BREASTS OF CHICKEN SAUTÉED WITH SHERRY WINE VINEGAR

Suprêmes de Volaille Sautés au Vinaigre de Malmsey

Serves 4

4 large half-breasts of chicken, boned, skin on, approximately 8
   ounces each
Salt and freshly ground white pepper to taste
2 tablespoons flour
2 tablespoons unsalted butter
2 tablespoons minced shallots
1 cup dry sherry
¼ cup + 2 tablespoons sherry wine vinegar
5 tablespoons unsalted butter

1 tablespoon chives, cut into 1″ lengths, for garnish

Season the chicken breasts with salt and pepper and dust with flour. Melt the butter in a sauté pan over medium-high heat. Add the chicken breasts, skin-side down (the skin-side, whether the skin is present or not, is the rounded side of the breast) and sauté until the skin is crisp. Reduce the heat to medium, turn the breasts over and sauté the other side (7–9 minutes total for both sides). Transfer the breasts to a warm platter.

Take the pan off the heat. Empty the pan of cooking fat and add the shallots, sherry and vinegar. Return the pan to medium-high heat and reduce the ingredients to ¼ cup. Off the heat, whisk the butter into the sauce, 1 tablespoon at a time, always waiting until the previous tablespoon has melted before adding the next one.

TO SERVE: Pour the sauce over the chicken breasts. Garnish with the chopped chives.

Roast Goose with Caraway Sauce

Oie Rôtie, Sauce Carvi

Serves 6

1 young 7–9 pound goose, whole
Salt and freshly ground white pepper to taste
1½ cups onions, diced into ½" pieces
2 tablespoons caraway seeds
4 cups veal stock (See recipe on page 30.)

To prepare the goose for roasting, remove any excess skin or fat at the openings of the neck and tail cavities. Clip the wings at the first joint (closest to the body). Season the cavity with salt and pepper.

To truss the goose, place it breast-up atop a 4' length of butcher's twine. The tail cavity should be facing toward you. The twine should be running under the front third of the goose, emerging in equal lengths from 2 spots just forward of the wings. Lift and cross the 2 lengths of twine as though you were going to wrap a package: one string should pin the right wing against the goose's body, cross the breast diagonally and knot itself around the left leg; the other piece of twine should pin the left wing against the body, cross the breast and secure itself to the right leg. Tie the drumsticks and the tail together in a tight little bundle, closing the tail cavity. Snip off any excess twine.

Preheat oven to 375 degrees.

Prick the skin of the goose all over with a sharp roasting fork, especially around the fatty thigh area. The holes allow the melted subcutaneous fat to escape during roasting.

Place the goose on its side and roast for 1¾ hours. After the first 30 minutes of roasting, turn the goose to its other side. After the second 30 minutes, turn the goose breast-up, pour off the fat in the bottom of the pan and add the onions and caraway seeds. Complete the roasting. Test the goose for doneness by pricking it with a metal skewer at the thigh joint. It's done when the juices run clear yellow, not pink.

While the goose is roasting, bring 4 cups of veal stock to a boil in a saucepan over medium-high heat. Lower the heat to medium and cook until the stock has reduced by half.

Remove the goose from the oven and allow it to repose for 15 minutes before carving. Cover it loosely with foil to keep it warm.

Preheat the broiler.

Discard the fat from the roasting pan. Save the onions and caraway seeds and set them aside in a saucepan. Set the roasting pan over medium-high heat. Add the reduced veal stock. Use a rubber spatula to loosen the caramelized particles of juices stuck to the pan.

When all the particles have dissolved, transfer the juices to the saucepan containing the onions and caraway seeds and let simmer for 20 minutes, or until reduced to 1½ cups. Strain the sauce and keep warm.

TO SERVE: Untruss the goose and carve the breast, thighs and leg meat off the bones, being careful to leave the skin intact. Cut the meat into large chunks and arrange on an oven-proof serving platter. Pass the platter under the broiler for a few minutes to crisp the skin. Serve the caraway sauce on the side.

CHAPTER 6

MEAT

Far more than any other category of entrée, the deft presentation of our meat dishes depends on the training and skill of our service staff. All Dining Room entrées are presented on silver platters to their respective tables, then put on plates in front of the diners. Quite a few of our meat dishes require a sophisticated knowledge of carving and cooking. Rack of lamb must be trimmed and portioned into chops. Chateaubriand must be sliced. In the case of *steak au poivre*, the captain sautés the meat, flames it with Cognac and then finishes the sauce under the eyes of the person who will be eating it. The Ritz-Carlton is the last hotel in Boston to provide this kind of service, a standard that at one time was observed by all first-class hotels. Certainly, part of the experience of eating here is enjoying a demonstration of tableside skill originating in the nineteenth century.

All the more reason, then, that our meat dishes should be superior. On a busy night we serve more than 1,500 entrées, the lion's share of which are meat. In the course of a year, I test approximately 200 different meat entrées. We treasure our meat purveyors, and I encourage you to seek a good butcher for your own cuts of beef, especially the expensive ones. You'll find that a relationship with a butcher can be invaluable when you want to put a really special dinner together at the last minute. In February of 1978, when forecasters began predicting heavy snow for Boston, we placed a last-minute order with a packing house that had been supplying us for thirty-nine years. The farsighted purveyor sent us enough meat for a month. The heavy snowfall turned into the blizzard of '78, trapping guests and employees in the hotel for three days. There are still people who visit the hotel and remember the weekend they survived on prime rib.

My earliest memory of meat dates back to when I was three-and-a-half years old. I remember sitting on the kitchen counter, watching my grandmother prepare *hasenpfeffer*, German rabbit stew. My grandmother gave me a taste, and to my surprise I crunched down on something that was as hard as a ball bearing. My grandfather had shot the rabbit, and in cleaning it had missed some of the buckshot. A dangerous business, eating meat. To this day I chew gingerly, a wary carnivore.

An increased awareness of the relationship between diet and health has made many Americans curtail their intake of red meat. A decade ago, veal entrées took a back seat to heavier selections like lamb and beef. Now we see an increased preference not only for veal, but lighter fare in general, like chicken and fish. With one exception—venison.

Deer meat had a special place in my family's diet. My father was not a sport hunter—we counted on the annual buck for the same reasons that we grew our own vegetables and raised our own chickens: to ease the cost of feeding an extended family that included all four grandparents. My father butchered the deer himself, and I can quite honestly say that my first steaks were wild venison. A special Sunday dinner was *sauerbraten*, pot roast with juniper berries made from venison top round.

In America, wild venison usually comes from a species of white-tailed deer. The venison we serve at The Ritz-Carlton, Boston actually comes from a slightly different animal—rather *two* animals. For the most part, we use European fallow deer raised on range farms in New Zealand. Fallow deer has a milder, less gamy flavor than white-tail, and its flesh, while extremely lean, is not as sinewy. From time to time we also use axis deer, range-farmed in Texas, similar in taste and texture to fallow. Venison has grown so popular that we currently import about fifty pounds a week. In terms of health, if red meat is danger-ous, then the intense purple color of deer meat would seem to signal a veritable minefield of hazardous fat. In reality, quite the opposite is true. Venison has between one-third and one-half the cholesterol content of its equivalent in grain-fed beef, an encouraging note in times when we are warned about the perils of eating those things we love the most.

Pepper Steak Flamed with Cognac

Entrecôte au Poivre Flambé

Serves 2

1½ cups veal stock (See recipe on page 30.)
2 tablespoons black peppercorns
2 sirloin steaks (10 ounces each)
Salt to taste
1 tablespoon unsalted butter
2 tablespoons finely chopped shallots
¼ cup + 2 tablespoons Cognac

2 sprigs watercress, for garnish

Bring the veal stock to a boil in a heavy-bottomed saucepan over high heat. Reduce the heat to medium and simmer until the stock has reduced by half (about 15 minutes). Remove the pan from heat and cover.

Rock a heavy-bottomed pan over the peppercorns to crush them.

Season the steaks with salt and roll them in the peppercorns, coating evenly.

Melt the butter in a large, heavy-bottomed sauté pan over medium-high heat. Sauté the steaks on both sides to the desired point of doneness (4–5 minutes per side for medium-rare). Transfer the steaks to a platter and keep warm.

Add the shallots to the pan and sauté over medium-high heat for 1 minute. Remove the pan from heat, add the Cognac and return the pan to the heat. Cook for 1 minute, add the reduced veal stock and allow the sauce to simmer until it has reduced by half. Season with salt.

TO SERVE: Pour the sauce over the steaks, garnish with fresh watercress and serve immediately.

LOIN OF VENISON WITH PEPPERCORNS AND LINGONBERRIES

Médaillons de Chevreuil au Poivre

Serves 4

8 venison medallions (3 ounces each)
1 cup veal stock (See recipe on page 30.)
1 teaspoon juniper berries
1 orange
2 tablespoons black peppercorns
Salt to taste
1 tablespoon unsalted butter
½ cup lingonberries

2 tablespoons chives, cut into ½" lengths, for garnish

Strictly speaking, a medallion (or *médaillon*) is a term used in French cuisine to describe a round piece of meat cut from the loin or tenderloin. Depending on the type of meat, medallions usually weigh 2–3 ounces apiece. In America, fillets cut from the loin or tenderloin are the closest equivalents. A butcher dealing in high-quality meats like loin of veal, lamb or venison will usually be willing to prepare them for you.

Bring the veal stock to a boil in a saucepan over high heat. Reduce the heat to medium, add the juniper berries and simmer for 10 minutes. Strain the stock and reserve.

This recipe calls for orange zest, the colored outer rind of the fruit. The easiest way of preparing it is to use a zesting tool, a small peeler made expressly for scraping the skin off citrus fruit. A good kitchen supply house will be able to provide you with one. Failing that, you can use a potato peeler. Try to cut wide swatches of skin, taking care to leave the white, pithy part of the rind attached to the fruit. Scrape any remaining pith off the zest or it will give the sauce a bitter flavor. Strip the orange of its zest. If you're using a peeler, slice the skin into narrow julienne strips ¹⁄₁₆" wide, approximately 1" long. Cut enough skin to make 2 tablespoons of julienned orange zest.

Blanch the zest in boiling water for 30 seconds, then rinse immediately under cold running water. Drain and set aside.

Rock a heavy-bottomed saucepan over the peppercorns to crack them.

Roll the venison fillets in the crushed peppercorns. The suggested quantity of peppercorns will partially cover the meat. Use more or less, according to your taste. Season the fillets with salt.

Melt the butter in a large, heavy-bottomed sauté pan over medium-high heat. Sauté the venison fillets on each side, 2–4 minutes per side, depending on how well done you prefer your meat. Venison, even farmed venison, is extremely lean. I suggest you cook it no more than 2½–3 minutes per side (for medium-rare), or you'll risk drying it out. Transfer the cooked fillets to a warmed serving platter.

Add the veal stock to the sauté pan. As the stock comes to a boil, scrape the pan to dissolve any caramelized bits of meat juice. Add the zest and lingonberries. Reduce the sauce until it thickens slightly, enough to lightly coat the back of a spoon.

TO SERVE: Pour the sauce directly over the venison fillets, garnish with chopped chives and serve immediately.

SAUTÉED VEAL WITH PROSCIUTTO AND SAGE

Médaillons de Veau au Jambon de Parme et Sauge

Serves 4

8 veal medallions (2½ ounces each)
6 ounces dried porcini mushrooms
2 cups veal stock (See recipe on page 30.)
1 stick + 2 tablespoons unsalted butter
Salt and freshly ground black pepper to taste
8 fresh sage leaves
1 cup flour
16 paper-thin slices of prosciutto ham
1 tablespoon minced shallots
¼ cup dry white wine
½ teaspoon finely chopped fresh sage

Strictly speaking, a medallion (or *médaillon*) is a term used in French cuisine to describe a round piece of meat cut from the loin or tenderloin. Depending on the type of meat, medallions usually weigh 2–3 ounces apiece. In America, fillets cut from the loin or tenderloin are the closest equivalents. A butcher dealing in high-quality meats like loin of veal, lamb or venison will usually be willing to prepare them for you. In this recipe, slightly less expensive alternatives to medallions are readily available veal cutlets.

Place the dried mushrooms in a bowl, cover with warm water and allow them to soak for 1 hour. Drain the mushrooms, saving the soaking liquid, and set aside. Strain the liquid through a fine sieve and refrigerate it for the next time you make rice, or any other dish that you'd like to enhance with the smoky flavor of wild mushrooms. If the mushrooms are not already sliced, slice them now, ¼" thick.

Bring the veal stock to a boil in a heavy-bottomed saucepan over high heat. Reduce the heat to medium and simmer until the stock has reduced to ¼ cup (about 30 minutes). The highly reduced veal stock, known as *glace de viande*, will have a syrupy texture. Remove the pan from the heat.

Place each medallion between 2 sheets of plastic wrap. Pound the veal with a heavy-bottomed sauce pan or flat meat tenderizer until each piece is ⅛" thick and 2½" in diameter. Be careful not to tear the flesh.

Clarify 1 stick of butter by melting it in a small pan over low heat. Skim the froth of casein that rises to the surface, then spoon out the clear yellow liquid (clarified butter) without disturbing the layer of whey in the bottom of the pan. Save ¼ cup of clarified butter for this recipe. Refrigerate any extra for future use.

Season the cutlets with salt and pepper and press 1 sage leaf into the center of each cutlet. Dredge the cutlets in flour, shaking off any excess, being careful not to dislodge the sage leaf.

Heat half the clarified butter in a large, heavy-bottomed sauté pan over high heat. Sauté half the cutlets. Do not crowd the pan. Cook each cutlet for approximately 30 seconds on each side. The veal should remain tender to the touch. Transfer the first batch of cutlets to a warmed serving platter. Add the remaining clarified butter to the pan and sauté the second batch of cutlets. Transfer the second batch of cutlets to the serving platter.

Lower the heat to medium high, add the prosciutto and sauté until just heated (about 20 seconds). Remove the pan from the heat. Alternate slices of veal and prosciutto on the serving platter.

Return the pan to medium-high heat. Add the sliced porcini and shallots and cook until the mushrooms are tender (3–4 minutes). Remove the pan from the heat and pour off any excess fat.

Add the white wine and return the pan to the heat. As the wine comes to a boil, scrape the sides of the pan to dissolve any bits of caramelized cooking juice. Add the glace de viande and chopped sage. Reduce the heat to low and swirl in the remaining 2 tablespoons of butter, 1 tablespoon at a time. Season with salt and pepper, but be careful— glace de viande and prosciutto are often very salty so you may not need to add any salt at all.

TO SERVE: Pour the sauce over the veal cutlets and serve immediately.

ROAST LOIN OF PORK WITH GLAZED-ONION GRAVY AND APPLES

Carré de Porc aux Oignons et Pommes

Serves 6

1 large Spanish onion
4 firm-textured apples (such as Granny Smith)
1 loin pork roast with rib bones, approximately 4 pounds (Ask your
    butcher to remove the back bone and to tie the roast so it holds
    its shape during cooking.)
2 tablespoons olive oil
Salt and freshly ground black pepper to taste
1½ teaspoons finely chopped fresh thyme (or 1 teaspoon dried)
1½ teaspoons finely chopped fresh marjoram (or ½ teaspoon
    dried)
2 tablespoons flour
½ cup dry white wine
½ cup applejack or sweet apple cider
3 cups veal stock (See recipe on page 30.)

Preheat oven to 350 degrees.

Cut the onion in half through the root end, and then into ⅛″ thick slices along the grain. Core and peel the apples, then slice them ⅛″ thick. Scatter the onions and apples in the roasting pan.

Brush the roast with the oil, season with salt and pepper and sprinkle with the herbs. Place the loin directly on top of the onion-apple mixture and roast for approximately 2 hours, checking frequently. If the onions or apples are becoming too browned, add water, ¼ cup at a time, to the roasting pan. The loin is done when its internal temperature reaches 150 degrees on a meat thermometer. Remove the loin from the pan, place it on a carving board and cover loosely with foil to keep it warm.

Heat the apples and onions, still in the roasting pan, over medium heat, stirring frequently, making sure all the onions are browned. Sprinkle with the flour and cook for 5 minutes, stirring frequently. Add the wine and applejack or cider, scraping the pan with a spatula to loosen and dissolve any bits of caramelized meat juice. Cook for 1 minute. Add the stock and allow the sauce to boil until it thickens enough to coat the back of a spoon (10–15 minutes). Season with salt and pepper.

TO SERVE: Bone and slice the loin. Arrange the slices on a warmed platter. Serve the gravy in a warmed sauce boat.

Sweetbreads with Pears and Rosemary

Ris de Veau aux Poires et Romarin

Serves 2

POACHING THE SWEETBREADS

½ cup onions, chopped into ½″ pieces
½ cup celery, chopped into ½″ pieces
½ cup carrots, chopped into ½″ pieces
2 bay leaves, whole
2 tablespoons white distilled vinegar
2 teaspoons salt
1 tablespoon black peppercorns
1 pound fresh sweetbreads

SAUTÉING THE SWEETBREAD MEDALLIONS

1½ cups veal stock (See recipe on page 30.)
2 fresh pears
1 lemon
Salt and freshly ground white pepper to taste
¼ cup flour
2 tablespoons unsalted butter
2 tablespoons minced shallots
1 teaspoon finely chopped fresh rosemary (or ½ teaspoon dried)
½ cup sauternes
¾ cup heavy cream

2 sprigs fresh rosemary, for garnish

POACHING THE SWEETBREADS: Bring 1 quart of water and all the poaching ingredients, except the sweetbreads, to a boil in a heavy-bottomed saucepan over high heat. Lower the heat to medium and simmer for 15 minutes. Rinse the raw sweetbreads under cold water and add them to the pan. If necessary, lower the heat even further—the poaching liquid should be barely simmering. Simmer for 20 minutes, or until the sweetbreads feel firm, but not rubbery. Remove from the stock and let cool. Discard the poaching liquid.

After the sweetbreads have cooled, remove all fatty tissue and fine membranes. Refrigerate until well chilled. Slicing on the bias, cut the sweetbreads into medallions ½″ thick.

SAUTÉING THE SWEETBREADS AND MAKING THE SAUCE: Bring the veal stock to a boil in a heavy-bottomed saucepan over high heat. Reduce the heat to medium and simmer until the stock has reduced by half (about 15 minutes). Remove the pan from the heat and cover.

Peel, core and slice the pears ¼″ thick. Place them in a bowl and cover with water. Squeeze the juice of the lemon into the water to prevent the pears from discoloring.

Season the sweetbreads with salt and pepper, dust with flour and shake off any excess. Melt 1 tablespoon of butter in a large, heavy-bottomed sauté pan over medium heat. Add the sweetbreads and sauté on both sides until golden brown and slightly crisp (about 5 minutes per side). Transfer the cooked sweetbreads to a serving platter and keep warm.

Add the remaining tablespoon of butter to the pan, add the shallots and chopped rosemary and sauté for 1 minute. Off the heat, add the sauternes, then return the pan to the heat. As the wine comes to a boil, use a spatula to scrape the sides of the pan, dissolving any bits of caramelized meat juice. Add the reduced veal stock and heavy cream and continue to cook until the mixture has reduced by half.

Drain the pears on paper towels and pat dry. Add them to the pan and sauté for 1 minute.

TO SERVE: Pour the hot sauce over the sweetbreads. Garnish with the sprigs of fresh rosemary and serve immediately.

ROAST BEEF HASH

Hachis de Boeuf Rôti

Serves 6

Hash was once considered the last word in fashionable light fare. In the thirties, when The Ritz-Carlton, Boston had a rooftop nightclub, chicken hash was far and away the most popular late night entrée. Roast beef hash, however, has proved more enduring, especially when paired with eggs for a hearty breakfast. We use about fifty pounds of roast beef a week in its preparation. And chicken hash? After trying to revive it—and failing to sell a single order over the course of an entire week—I decided some dishes are best left as historical curiosities.

HASH

1 cup veal stock (See recipe on page 30.)
1½ pounds russet potatoes
5 tablespoons unsalted butter
1 cup onions, diced into ¼″ pieces
1½ pounds cooked roast beef, preferably prime rib, cut into ½″ cubes
Salt and freshly ground white pepper to taste

POACHING THE EGGS

1 tablespoon white distilled vinegar
2 teaspoons salt
6 large eggs

MAKING THE HASH: Bring the veal stock to a boil in a heavy-bottomed saucepan over high heat. Reduce the heat to medium and simmer until the stock has reduced to ½ cup (about 15 minutes). Remove the pan from the heat and cover.

Bring 4 cups of water to a boil. Add the potatoes and cook until they can be easily pierced with a knife. Rinse under cold water. After they've cooled, peel and dice them into ½″ cubes. You should have 3 cups of diced potatoes.

Melt 3 tablespoons of butter in a large, heavy-bottomed sauté pan over medium-high heat. Add the onions and sauté until golden. Add the cooked roast beef and sauté until well-browned. Add the potatoes and mix well. Add the reduced veal stock and season with salt and pepper. Remove the pan from heat and allow the mixture to cool.

Form the hash mixture into oval patties, 5″ x 3″ in diameter and 1″ thick.

Melt 2 tablespoons of butter in a large, non-stick sauté pan over medium heat. Sauté the patties on both sides until crisp and well-browned. Transfer the patties to a platter and keep warm.

POACHING THE EGGS: Fill a large sauté pan with 2″ of water. Add the vinegar and salt. Bring to a boil over high heat. Reduce the heat to medium-low (the water should be barely simmering). Break an egg into a small bowl without rupturing the yolk. Carefully tip the egg out of the bowl into the simmering water. Repeat with remaining eggs. If necessary, cook the eggs in batches. Poach the eggs for 4 minutes.

TO SERVE: Transfer the patties to warmed individual plates and top each with a poached egg.

ROAST RACK OF LAMB

Carré d'Agneau Dijonnaise

Serves 2

½ cup fresh bread crumbs
1 teaspoon finely chopped fresh thyme (or ½ teaspoon dried)
2 tablespoons finely chopped parsley
2 teaspoons minced garlic
2 tablespoons olive oil
1 rack of lamb (approximately 1½ pounds—make sure your rack
    has 8 chops, and have your butcher "french" the bones, i.e., strip
    the fat and gristle from the final 3″ of each bone)
Salt and freshly ground black pepper to taste
2 tablespoons Dijon mustard

Preheat oven to 400 degrees.

To prepare the crumb topping, put the bread crumbs in a mixing bowl, add the thyme, parsley, garlic and 1 tablespoon of olive oil and mix well.

Season the rack with salt and pepper. Heat the remaining tablespoon of olive oil in a large, heavy-bottomed sauté pan over medium-high heat. Sear the rack and then remove it from the pan. Let it cool for 5 minutes.

Wrap the exposed bones with aluminum foil so they don't burn during the roasting. Coat the rack, except the bones, with the Dijon mustard, and then press the crumb mixture evenly over the mustard.

Put the rack in a pan and roast for 25 minutes (for medium-rare) or until a meat thermometer registers an internal temperature of 122 degrees. Remove the rack from the oven and let it repose 10 minutes before serving.

TO SERVE: Remove the aluminum foil from the bones. Slice the rack into individual chops and arrange 4 overlapping chops on each plate.

Hungarian-Style Veal Goulash

Goulasch de Veau

Serves 6

8 cups veal stock (See recipe on page 30.)
2 pounds veal stew meat, well-trimmed, cut into 1½″ cubes
4 cups chicken stock (See recipe on page 31.)
2 tablespoons vegetable oil
1 cup onions, sliced ¼″ thick
2 cups red peppers, diced into ¼″ pieces
1 cup green peppers, diced into ¼″ pieces
1 tablespoon minced garlic
2 teaspoons finely chopped fresh thyme (or 1½ teaspoons dried)
1 tablespoon caraway seeds
2 teaspoons finely chopped fresh marjoram (or 1 teaspoon dried)
2 teaspoons freshly ground black pepper
2 tablespoons paprika
¾ cup tomato purée
1 bottle strong dark beer
Salt and freshly ground black pepper to taste

Bring the veal stock to a boil in a heavy-bottomed saucepan over high heat. Reduce the heat to medium and simmer until the stock has reduced to 4 cups (about 20 minutes). Remove the pan from the heat and cover.

Wash the veal cubes under cold running water. Pat dry with paper towels.

Combine the veal cubes and chicken stock in a large, heavy-bottomed saucepan and bring to a boil over high heat. Lower the heat to medium and simmer for 20 minutes, skimming the foam of impurities that rises to the surface of the stock. Scoop the veal out of the stock and cool. Save this stock for another use.

Heat the oil in a large Dutch oven over medium-high heat. When the oil starts to smoke, add the onions, red and green peppers, garlic, thyme, caraway seeds, marjoram and 2 teaspoons of black pepper. Sauté the vegetables, stirring constantly, until they start to brown (8–10 minutes). Add the paprika, tomato purée and beer. Lower the heat to medium and cook for 2 minutes. Add the reduced veal stock and cook for another 20 minutes.

Remove the pot from the heat and purée the sauce in a food processor. Do it in several batches, taking care not to fill the food processor with too much hot sauce at one time. The vegetables will thicken the sauce slightly. After you've finished, taste the sauce and season with salt and pepper.

Place the cooked veal in a clean Dutch oven and add the sauce. Bring to a boil and immediately lower the heat to medium. Allow the mixture to simmer for 20 minutes, or until the veal is tender.

FILLET OF BEEF WITH GREEN PEPPERCORN SAUCE

Médaillons de Boeuf au Poivre Vert

Serves 4

1½ cups veal stock (See recipe on page 30.)
8 beef medallions (4 ounces each), cut from well-trimmed beef
    tenderloin
Salt and freshly ground white pepper to taste
2 tablespoons unsalted butter
2 tablespoons minced shallots
2 tablespoons green peppercorns
¼ cup + 2 tablespoons Madeira
½ cup heavy cream

4 sprigs fresh thyme, for garnish

Strictly speaking, a medallion (or *médaillon*) is a term used in French cuisine to describe a round piece of meat cut from the loin or tenderloin. Depending on the type of meat, medallions usually weigh 2–3 ounces apiece, although in this recipe you're using slightly heavier ones. In America, fillets cut from the loin or tenderloin are the closest equivalents. A butcher dealing in high-quality meats like loin of veal, lamb or venison will usually be willing to prepare them for you.

Bring the veal stock to a boil in a heavy-bottomed saucepan over high heat. Reduce the heat to medium and simmer until the stock has reduced to ¾ cup (about 15 minutes). Remove the pan from the heat and cover.

Season the medallions with salt and pepper.

Melt the butter over medium-high heat in a heavy-bottomed sauté pan large enough to hold the medallions without crowding. If necessary, cook them in 2 batches. Sauté the medallions on both sides to the desired point of doneness (2 minutes per side for rare). Transfer them to a platter and keep warm.

Lower the heat to medium and add the shallots and green peppercorns. Sauté for 1 minute, then add the Madeira. Continue cooking for 1 minute.

Add the reduced veal stock and cream. Allow the sauce to simmer until it has reduced by half. Season with salt and pepper.

TO SERVE: Pour the sauce over the medallions and garnish with sprigs of fresh thyme.

CHAPTER 7

SAUCES

The Ritz-Carlton *saucier* oversees a daily production of at least sixteen different classical French sauces (down from a minimum of twenty-two, when I was promoted to the job). Our kitchen has never hired a saucier from outside the restaurant—with its enormous responsibility, the position requires a person who can be cultivated for the job, nurtured and instructed until he or she is ready. After promotion, the saucier goes through a three-month apprenticeship to insure that the sauces conform exactly to the chef's tastes. The saucier sheds quite a few tears during this period—if I taste a sauce and judge it to be inferior, the saucier throws it away and begins again, from scratch. Severe standards guarantee that no matter how complex the preparation, the end result always enhances a dish. A good sauce has the power to elevate a mediocre piece of steak or chicken, but a bad sauce can positively destroy a rack of lamb or loin of veal that could have quite properly stood on its own merits.

In preparing stock for sauces, we use approximately 150 pounds of veal bones and 100 of chicken bones each day; fish stock, made three times a week, requires its own 100 pounds of fish bones. The movement toward pan sauces or variations on *beurre blanc*, a light butter sauce made from a reduction of white wine, lemon juice, shallots and butter, has lessened the labor of sauce-making. A little technique and advance preparation can enable the home cook to whisk together a tasty sauce which, if not quite the equal of that produced in the professional kitchen, has also not required the hours of skimming and hawk-like attention to temperature so that the sauce simmers and never boils.

More than in any other chapter, the recipes gathered in the next few pages will provide you with a range of self-expression—sauces taking a few minutes or several hours. For some home cooks, simple mayonnaise is a discovery and a delight, especially when additional spices, herbs or a tablespoon or two of puréed vegetable (red bell pepper, for example) added to the basic recipe produce an entirely different sauce. Others will want to try the more complex offerings. People frown with impatience when I tell them that, at heart, no one who wants to make a classical French sauce, by which I mean a sauce in the tradition of Escoffier, can concern himself with time. "How can you say that?" they cry. "Even professional chefs have to make sure that sauces are finished before the restaurant's evening service." True, but professional quality sauces take time for two reasons—they require stocks which can take four or five hours to make, and in the case of flour-thickened sauces, they require cooking time to eliminate the starchy flavor. Let me add that the home cook has a host of much quicker alternatives to flour-based sauces. Stock keeps well refrigerated; an ample supply will repay you with many "quick" pan sauces made only from wine or water, stock and butter.

In my own family, pan sauces accompanied all meat dishes. My mother thickened the pan juices with butter or, in the case of certain stock-based sauces, with pumpernickel bread. An atypical French proverb modestly asserts that the best sauce is a hearty appetite, but I haven't met the diner yet who'd say, "Hold the sauce, please, my appetite's enough."

CUMBERLAND SAUCE

Sauce Cumberland

Yields about 2 cups

Cumberland sauce is a traditional English accompaniment to cold game. The sauce is based on a reduction of herbs and spices, orange juice, port and currant jelly. Refrigerated, it will keep for weeks, making it a nice condiment to have on hand for cold meat leftovers or pâté.

1½ cups red currant jelly
1 lemon
2–3 oranges (enough for 1 cup of juice)
1 cup port
1 tablespoon black peppercorns
1 bay leaf, whole
2 teaspoons finely chopped fresh thyme (or 1 teaspoon dried)
2 tablespoons minced shallots
1 tablespoon finely chopped fresh ginger

Strain the red currant jelly through a fine sieve into a mixing bowl and set aside.

This recipe calls for lemon and orange zest, the colored outer rind of the fruit. The easiest way to prepare it is to use a zesting tool, a small peeler made expressly for scraping the skin off citrus fruit. A good kitchen supply house will be able to provide you with one. Failing that, you can use a potato peeler. Try to cut wide swatches of skin, taking care to leave the white, pithy part of the rind attached to the fruit. Scrape any remaining pith off the zest or it will give the sauce a bitter flavor. Strip the lemon and 1 orange of their zest. If you used a potato peeler, cut the swatches of skin into narrow julienne strips $\frac{1}{16}''$ wide, approximately 1″ long. Cut enough skin from each rind to make 1 tablespoon each of julienned lemon and orange zest.

Blanch the zest in boiling water for 30 seconds, then rinse immediately under cold running water. Drain and add to the mixing bowl with the currant jelly.

Cut the oranges in half, including the peeled one, and squeeze out the juice. You should have 1 cup of juice. Pour the juice into a heavy-bottomed saucepan. Cut the lemon in half and squeeze 2 tablespoons of juice into the saucepan. Add the port, the peppercorns, bay leaf, thyme, shallots and fresh ginger to the saucepan. Bring the mixture to a boil over high heat. Lower the heat to medium and let the mixture reduce by half. Strain into the mixing bowl with the currant jelly and the zest. Blend everything well. Let the sauce stand overnight, covered and refrigerated, to develop its full flavor.

FRESH HERB CREAM

Sauce Verte

Yields about 3 cups

Sauce verte usually accompanies cold fish or poultry, but I find it also makes an outstanding salad dressing or a nice foil to grilled shrimp.

1 tablespoon chives, washed and chopped
½ cup watercress, picked of stems, washed
¼ cup parsley, picked of stems, washed
½ cup coarsely chopped spinach leaves
1 tablespoon finely chopped fresh tarragon
1 tablespoon finely chopped fresh chervil
1 tablespoon lemon juice
1 tablespoon white distilled vinegar
½ cup sour cream
1 cup mayonnaise (See recipe on page 105.)
1 teaspoon sugar
¼ cup heavy cream
Salt and freshly ground white pepper to taste

Place all of the ingredients in a food processor and blend very well (about 4 minutes), pausing frequently to scrape the side of the bowl. The sauce will be vivid green and have bits of herbs suspended in it. Refrigerate the sauce overnight in a covered container to develop its full flavor.

DOVER SOLE
pages 50–51

FRESH CRAB WITH LINGUINI, TOMATO-BASIL VINAIGRETTE
pages 60–61

Swordfish with Mustard Cream and Jalapeños
page 58

Poached Salmon with Hollandaise Sauce
page 62

CHICKEN POT PIE

pages 65–66

PEPPER STEAK FLAMED WITH COGNAC

page 79

ROAST RACK OF LAMB (PLATED)
page 88

ROAST RACK OF LAMB (SERVED)

CREAMY COCKTAIL SAUCE

Sauce Louis

Yields about 2 cups

At first glance *sauce Louis* resembles Russian dressing, but the zip of horseradish and red bell peppers immediately puts the taste of this cocktail sauce in a field of its own. We serve it as a side dressing for cold poached seafood or poultry.

1¼ cups mayonnaise (See recipe on page 105.)
1 tablespoon prepared horseradish, squeezed of juice
2 tablespoons chili sauce
2 tablespoons ketchup
1 tablespoon red bell peppers, diced into ¼″ pieces
1 tablespoon green peppers, diced into ¼″ pieces
1 tablespoon minced shallots
1 tablespoon chives, cut into ¼″ lengths
1 tablespoon red wine vinegar
1 tablespoon vegetable oil
2 teaspoons paprika
1 teaspoon cayenne pepper
2 teaspoons sugar
Salt and freshly ground white pepper to taste

Combine all the ingredients in a mixing bowl and blend well. Let the sauce stand overnight, covered and refrigerated, to develop its full flavor.

COCKTAIL SAUCE

Sauce Cocktail

Yields about 1½ cups

½ cup ketchup
¾ cup chili sauce
3 tablespoons prepared horseradish, squeezed of juice
1 teaspoon Tabasco sauce
1 teaspoon Worcestershire sauce
1 tablespoon lemon juice

Combine all the ingredients in a mixing bowl and blend well. Let the sauce stand overnight, covered and refrigerated, to develop its full flavor.

HORSERADISH SAUCE

Crème Raifort

Yields about 1½ cups

Horseradish sauce is an interesting alternative to the traditional garnishes served with smoked salmon or whitefish. I also like this on cold roast beef.

1 cup sour cream
3 tablespoons prepared horseradish, squeezed of juice
1 tablespoon lemon juice
⅛ teaspoon cayenne pepper
Salt and freshly ground white pepper to taste

Combine all the ingredients in a mixing bowl and blend well. Let the sauce stand overnight, covered and refrigerated, to develop its full flavor.

CHAMPAGNE SAUCE

Sauce Champenoise

Yields about 1½ cups

Champagne sauce and *sauce vin blanc* are the two white wine fish sauces we use most frequently at the hotel. Champagne sauce is quite versatile, and after you become familiar with the recipe, you should try enhancing it with different fresh herbs, tomatoes or mushrooms.

4 cups fish stock (See recipe on page 32.)
2 teaspoons white peppercorns
1 cup + 2 tablespoons *brut* Champagne
2 tablespoons finely chopped shallots
1 sprig fresh thyme (or ½ teaspoon dried)
2 cups heavy cream
2 tablespoons unsalted butter, softened
Salt and freshly ground white pepper to taste

Bring the fish stock to a boil in a heavy-bottomed saucepan over high heat. Lower the heat to medium-high and simmer until the stock has reduced by half (about 30 minutes).

Rock a heavy-bottomed saucepan over the peppercorns to crush them, then put the peppercorns in the saucepan. Add 1 cup of Champagne, the shallots and the thyme. Bring the mixture to a boil over high heat. Lower the heat to medium and simmer until the liquid has reduced to 1 tablespoon. Be careful not to let everything boil away.

Add the fish stock and cream and bring everything back to a boil. Lower the heat to medium and continue cooking until the sauce reduces to 1½ cups. Skim off the foam of impurities that rises to the surface as the sauce reduces.

When the sauce has reduced, add the remaining 2 tablespoons of Champagne and remove the pan from the heat. Whisk the butter into the sauce, 1 tablespoon at a time. Season with salt and pepper. Strain the sauce through a fine sieve into a warm sauce boat.

I don't recommend refrigerating cream sauces because they tend to separate. However, there are those times when you have no choice. Warm the refrigerated sauce over very low heat, whisking occasionally. You can "fix" a broken sauce by putting it into a blender, but the texture will be slightly affected by the air introduced into the mixture.

WHITE WINE FISH SAUCE

Sauce Vin Blanc

Yields about 1½ cups

1 cup dry white wine
1 tablespoon minced shallots
1 teaspoon white peppercorns
1 small bay leaf, whole
¼ teaspoon finely chopped fresh thyme (or ⅛ teaspoon dried)
1 cup fish stock (See recipe on page 32.)
2 cups heavy cream
1 teaspoon arrowroot or cornstarch
1 tablespoon water
Salt and freshly ground white pepper to taste

Bring the white wine, shallots, peppercorns, bay leaf, thyme and fish stock to a boil in a heavy-bottomed saucepan over high heat. Lower the heat to medium and simmer until the stock has reduced to 1 cup (about 15 minutes). Add the heavy cream and continue to reduce until the mixture has thickened enough to lightly coat a spoon. Watch the cream closely so that it doesn't boil over.

Combine the arrowroot or cornstarch with 1 tablespoon of cold water. Blend into a smooth, runny mixture.

Increase the heat under the saucepan to medium-high. When the mixture begins to boil briskly, whisk the arrowroot or cornstarch mixture into the sauce, whisking constantly. Lower the heat and simmer the sauce for 3–4 minutes. Season with salt and pepper. Strain the sauce through a fine sieve into a warmed sauce boat.

I don't recommend refrigerating cream sauces because they tend to separate. However, there are those times when you have no choice. Warm the refrigerated sauce over very low heat, whisking occasionally. You can "fix" a broken sauce by putting it into a blender, but the texture will be slightly affected by the air introduced into the mixture.

MUSTARD SAUCE

Sauce Moutarde

Yields about 1¼ cups

This sauce gets its character from granular, whole-seed mustard instead of the commonly used Dijon style. Use it with broiled, grilled or pan-fried meats, or with roast chicken or duckling.

8 cups veal stock (See recipe on page 30.)
1 cup heavy cream
2 tablespoons Pommery mustard
2 tablespoons unsalted butter, softened
Salt and freshly ground white pepper to taste

Bring the stock to a boil in a heavy-bottomed saucepan over high heat. Lower the heat to medium-high and reduce the stock to 1½ cups, skimming off the foam of impurities that rises to the surface. Add the heavy cream and continue to cook until the sauce has reduced to 1¼ cups.

Take the pan off the heat, add the mustard and whisk in the butter, 1 tablespoon at a time. Season with salt and pepper. Pour the sauce into a warm sauce boat or reserve for other use. This sauce can be refrigerated without any problem. Just warm it gently over low heat before serving.

Red Wine and Shallot Sauce

Sauce Marchand de Vins

Yields about 1½ cups

8 cups veal stock (See recipe on page 30.)
1 teaspoon black peppercorns
2 cups dry red wine
2 tablespoons minced shallots
1 sprig fresh thyme (or ½ teaspoon dried)
1 bay leaf, whole
Salt and freshly ground white pepper to taste
1 tablespoon arrowroot or cornstarch
1 tablespoon water
2 tablespoons unsalted butter, softened

Bring the stock to a boil in a heavy-bottomed saucepan over high heat. Lower the heat to medium-high and reduce the stock to 1½ cups (about 45 minutes), skimming off the foam of impurities that rises to the surface. Remove the pan from the heat, cover, and keep the reduced stock warm.

Rock a heavy-bottomed saucepan over the peppercorns to crush them, then put the peppercorns in the saucepan with the red wine, shallots, thyme and bay leaf. Bring the mixture to a boil over high heat. Lower the heat to medium and simmer until the liquid has reduced to ½ cup. Add the reduced stock and continue to cook until the liquid has reduced to 1½ cups. Season with salt and pepper.

Combine the arrowroot or cornstarch with 1 tablespoon of water. Blend into a smooth, runny mixture.

Increase the heat under the saucepan to medium-high. When the sauce begins to boil briskly, add the arrowroot or cornstarch mixture, whisking constantly until it's completely absorbed. Lower the heat and simmer the sauce for 3–4 minutes.

Remove the pan from the heat. If you're going to use the sauce immediately, proceed directly to the next step; otherwise refrigerate the reduced wine-stock mixture, reheating the mixture when you intend to finish the sauce.

To finish the sauce, remove the pan from the heat and whisk in the butter, 1 tablespoon at a time. Strain the sauce through a fine sieve into a warmed sauce boat and serve.

HOLLANDAISE SAUCE

Sauce Hollandaise

Yields about 1½ cups

¾ pound unsalted butter
1 tablespoon black peppercorns
1 tablespoon white distilled vinegar
1 tablespoon water
2 teaspoons minced shallots
3 egg yolks, from large eggs
2 teaspoons lemon juice
⅛ teaspoon cayenne pepper
Salt to taste
Lemon juice to taste

Clarify the butter by melting it in a small pan over low heat. Skim the froth of casein that rises to the surface, then spoon out the clear yellow liquid (clarified butter) without disturbing the layer of whey in the bottom of the pan. Keep the clarified butter warm in a small covered pot, with the heat adjusted as low as possible.

Crush the black peppercorns by rocking a heavy-bottomed saucepan over them.

Simmer the crushed black peppercorns, vinegar, 1 tablespoon of water and shallots in a small saucepan over medium heat. Cook the mixture until it has reduced by half. Be careful—the mixture will reduce in only a few minutes. Using a fine sieve, strain the mixture into a stainless steel mixing bowl.

For this next step you may leave the mixture in the stainless steel mixing bowl or transfer it to the top part of a double boiler (as long as it's not aluminum). In a saucepan or bottom half of a double boiler bring 2″ of water to a gentle boil over medium heat. Set the mixing bowl or the top part of the double boiler over the water. Add the egg yolks, 2 teaspoons lemon juice and cayenne pepper to the mixing bowl. It's important that the water isn't boiling rapidly or the yolks will cook too quickly. Whisk the yolks continuously with a wire whip until they thicken and take on a white, frothy appearance. When the yolks reach this stage, remove the bowl from over the water and continue whisking for 2 minutes. This gives the yolks a chance to cool a bit and helps prevent accidental overcooking.

Begin whisking the clarified butter, drop by drop, into the egg yolk mixture. To insure a successful emulsion, add the first drops of butter very slowly. Once the eggs have absorbed about ¼ cup of butter you can begin adding it in a slow, steady stream, never stopping the whisking. If the sauce seems to be getting too thick, add a teaspoon of warm water. When you've added all the butter, taste the sauce and season with salt and lemon juice.

HOLLANDAISE-BASED SAUCES: There are dozens of variations on the basic butter and egg yolk combination. One of the most popular is *maltaise*. To make a maltaise sauce, simply substitute 1 tablespoon of orange juice for the 2 teaspoons of lemon juice, and add a tablespoon of finely-grated orange rind (just the orange part) to the strained vinegar reduction at the same time you add the orange juice.

BÉARNAISE SAUCE

Sauce Béarnaise

Yields about 1½ cups

¾ **pound unsalted butter**
1 **teaspoon black peppercorns**
2 **tablespoons white distilled vinegar**
2 **tablespoons water**
1 **teaspoon finely chopped fresh tarragon (or ½ teaspoon dried)**
1 **teaspoon finely chopped fresh chervil (or ½ teaspoon dried)**
2 **teaspoons minced shallots**
3 **egg yolks, from large eggs**
Salt to taste
Lemon juice to taste
2 **teaspoons parsley, finely chopped**

Clarify the butter by melting it in a small pan over low heat. Skim the froth of casein that rises to the surface, then spoon out the clear yellow liquid (clarified butter) without disturbing the layer of whey in the bottom of the pan. Keep the clarified butter warm in a small covered pot, with the heat adjusted as low as possible.

Crush the black peppercorns by rocking a heavy-bottomed saucepan over them.

Simmer the crushed black peppercorns, vinegar, water, tarragon, chervil and shallots in a small saucepan over medium heat. Cook the mixture until it has reduced by half. Be careful—the mixture will reduce in only a few minutes. Transfer the mixture, without straining, to a stainless steel mixing bowl.

For this next step you may leave the mixture in the stainless steel mixing bowl or transfer it to the top part of a double boiler (as long as it's not aluminum). In a saucepan or bottom half of a double boiler bring 2″ of water to a gentle boil over medium heat. Set the mixing bowl or the top part of the double boiler over the water. Add the egg yolks to the bowl. It's important that the water isn't boiling rapidly or the yolks will cook too quickly. Whisk the yolks continuously with a wire whip until they thicken and take on a white, frothy appearance. When the yolks reach this stage, remove the bowl from over the water and continue whisking for 2 minutes. This gives the yolks a chance to cool a bit and helps prevent accidental overcooking.

Begin whisking the clarified butter, drop by drop, into the egg yolk mixture. To insure a successful emulsion, add the first drops of butter very slowly . Once the eggs have ab-sorbed about ¼ cup of butter you can begin adding it in a slow steady stream, never stop-ping the whisking. If the sauce seems to be getting too thick, add a teaspoon of warm water. When you've added all the butter, taste the sauce and season with salt and lemon juice, then stir in the chopped parsley.

FOR SAUCE CHORON: Choron is a tomato-flavored version of béarnaise. To make it, follow the béarnaise recipe, adding 1 tablespoon of tomato paste to the vinegar reduction when you add the egg yolks.

WHITE AND RED WINE BUTTER SAUCES

Beurre Blanc et Beurre Rouge

Yields about 2 cups

Simple butter sauces are an elegant way to enhance a steak or piece of grilled fish, espe-cially at the last minute. If you want a lighter sauce, add less cream.

**2 cups dry white or red wine (depending on whether you want a
  white or red butter sauce)**
1 shallot, minced
**1 teaspoon minced fresh herb mixture (chervil, tarragon and thyme,
  in equal amounts)**
½ cup heavy cream
1 pound unsalted butter, cut into ½″ cubes, chilled
Salt and freshly ground white pepper to taste

Bring the wine, shallots and herbs to a boil in a heavy-bottomed saucepan over high heat. Lower the heat to medium and simmer the wine until it has reduced to ¼ cup. Add the heavy cream and again reduce to ¼ cup. Turn the heat to low and whisk in the butter, one cube at a time, emulsifying the butter with the reduction. *Do not boil! If the sauce boils, the emulsion will separate!* The finished consistency should be somewhere between light and heavy cream, a slightly thickened sauce that lightly coats the back of a spoon. Season with salt and pepper. Strain the sauce through a fine sieve into a warmed sauce boat.

Butter sauces will not keep refrigerated. You can, however, hold them for several hours in a warm water bath or in the top part of a double boiler with warm water underneath. Just be sure not to let the water boil.

Béchamel Sauce

Sauce Béchamel

Yields about 1½ cups

1 cup milk
1 cup light cream
2 tablespoons unsalted butter
2 tablespoons flour
1 bay leaf, whole
⅛ teaspoon freshly grated nutmeg
1 small onion, cut in half
Salt and freshly ground white pepper to taste

Combine the milk and cream in a saucepan and bring them to a boil over high heat. Remove the pan from the heat and cover, to keep the contents warm.

Melt the 2 tablespoons of butter in a heavy-bottomed saucepan over medium heat. Add the flour and cook for 2 minutes, stirring constantly so the butter doesn't brown. Now add the milk and cream mixture in a steady stream, whisking briskly until the mixture is well-blended. Add the remaining ingredients and reduce the heat to low. Allow the sauce to simmer for 10 minutes. A scum of protein from the flour will rise to the surface as the sauce simmers. Skim this off and strain the sauce through a fine sieve. Béchamel sauce should be refrigerated if you don't intend to use it immediately. To reheat the sauce, place it in a saucepan over low heat, stirring occasionally so the sauce doesn't burn.

MAYONNAISE

Sauce Mayonnaise

Yields about 4 cups

Mayonnaise is one of those preparations that always astound beginner cooks. It's such a basic ingredient to so many recipes that we take it for granted, like flour. At the hotel we use a high-quality commercial mayonnaise only in spicy recipes, when the seasonings are so dominant they obscure the difference between the commercial and homemade varieties. On the other hand, there's no substitute for a mayonnaise you've made yourself when you're making a subtle herb dressing to complement cold poached chicken or the delicate flavor of smoked trout fillets.

1 tablespoon sugar
2 teaspoons salt
½ teaspoon freshly ground white pepper
2 teaspoons dry mustard
4 egg yolks, from large eggs
3½ cups vegetable oil
¼ cup white distilled vinegar
2 tablespoons lemon juice

Combine the dry ingredients in a small bowl and set aside.

In a large mixing bowl, beat the egg yolks with a wire whisk until they start to foam. Add the dry ingredients and continue to beat for 2 minutes. Slowly dribble the oil into the egg mixture, drop by drop at first, beating constantly. The more slowly you add the oil and the more conscientious you are about constantly whisking, the greater your chances for a successful emulsion. Once the mixture begins to thicken (after you've added about ¼ cup of oil), you can add the oil in a slow steady stream. Occasionally stop to add a tablespoon of vinegar. Continue until both the oil and vinegar are used up.

Finish the mayonnaise with the lemon juice and season with additional salt and pepper, if necessary. If the sauce is too thick, it can be thinned with 1 or 2 tablespoons of warm water.

What to do if the mayonnaise breaks: Culinary lore is rife with superstition explaining why mayonnaise separates. Thunderstorms were long held responsible, as were pregnant women, who, it was believed, jinxed the eggs. Such fancies aside, mayonnaise breaks for two primary reasons: adding the oil too quickly or adding too much of it. If you add the oil too quickly the eggs don't have time to emulsify, and the result is a "broken" sauce—one that has separated into its constituent ingredients. If, however, your mayonnaise looks fine, but it breaks after you've set it aside for a few minutes, then you've added too much oil for the amount of egg yolk in your sauce. Broken mayonnaise (or hollandaise, or any of their numerous variants) is easily reconstituted. Simply put an egg yolk into a clean mixing bowl and beat it until it begins to foam, then *slowly* add your broken sauce to the new egg yolk, whisking constantly, always waiting until you've completely blended the egg yolk and sauce in the bowl before adding more sauce. Taste the mayonnaise and finish with more salt, pepper and lemon juice, if necessary.

CHAPTER 8

VEGETABLES

Have you ever eaten an otherwise memorable meal spoiled by poorly cooked vegetables? Unless a cook exercises care, vegetables will inevitably find their way back into the kitchen, a forlorn mess awaiting the attention of the dishwasher. Mastery of vegetable cookery requires a light touch, and an eye for drama—without overwhelming the entrée.

We'll never know how Escoffier would have reacted to the roster of exotic vegetables now served at The Ritz-Carlton, Boston, or what he would have made of their year-round availability. Leeks, for example, used to appear only in the spring; Belgian endive a little later. Now we see leeks (though not the baby ones) even in the dead of winter, and endive, which had one European season, is now flown in from Chile, and most recently, grown hydroponically in New York State. Undoubtedly he would have approved of the recent trend to preserve as much of the vegetables' original taste and texture in the finished product as possible—hence the preference for lightly steamed green beans or grilled eggplant; and lightly blanched broccoli, brilliant green, scooped from the boiling water before it fades to the color of an army uniform.

I've found that the best ideas for vegetables often come, naturally enough, from those cultures where meat is expensive or used sparingly. The idea for one of our vegetarian entrées, spicy bean curd with bean sprouts, hot chili paste and peppers, is actually an amalgam of several dishes I tasted in China. The Chinese treat vegetables with enormous respect. In Canton my wife and I dined in the Gwanjo Restaurant with four other restaurant professionals from the West. Seating almost 2,000, the restaurant had five levels filled with tables accommodating ten or more persons. The Chinese family sitting across from us informed us of the local custom of sharing dinners between parties, an opportunity my wife gladly accepted when two of the dishes we ordered turned out to be deep-fried pork belly and stir-fried frogs (whole frogs cut in quarters, not frogs' legs). In exchange, we received a healthy portion of braised baby bok choy with oyster sauce. Mature bok choy, a Chinese cabbage, typically shows up in produce markets as a long, narrow head, similar in shape and size to romaine lettuce. But this was a treat! Each of the baby bok choy, served whole, was about the size of my thumb, and their sweet flavor, not yet full-blown into the taste of cabbage, complemented the light tang of the oyster sauce. Whenever our produce suppliers manage to trap a case or two of these prized baby cabbages, we serve bok choy as a special side dish on the menu of The Dining Room.

I like to roast some of the sturdier vegetables—large carrots and potatoes, for example. Roasting works equally well with other root vegetables like parsnips, or even with some of the squashes, especially if you can add a spoonful of goose or duck fat to the roasting pan.

Belgian Endive

Chicorée Sautée Meunière

Serves 4

4 large Belgian endives
1 tablespoon unsalted butter
1 tablespoon lemon juice
Salt to taste
1 cup chicken stock (See recipe on page 31.)
3 tablespoons salted butter
½ cup flour
Freshly ground white pepper to taste

1 tablespoon finely chopped parsley, for garnish
4 lemon wedges, for garnish

Cut the endives in half lengthwise and wash them under cold running water. Trim the stems, if necessary, taking care to keep the leaves attached.

Melt the unsalted butter over medium heat in a sauté pan large enough to hold the endives in a single layer. Add the endives, lemon juice, salt and chicken stock. Increase the heat to high and bring to a boil. Reduce the heat to medium and simmer until the endives are tender and can be easily pierced with a knife (10–15 minutes). Transfer the endives to a rack to drain and cool. Discard the cooking liquid.

Melt the salted butter over medium heat in a sauté pan large enough to hold the endives in a single layer. Dust the endives with flour and white pepper, shaking off any excess, then straighten the endives into their natural shape. Add the endives to the pan and sauté on each side until they're golden brown (about 5 minutes). Remove them from the pan and drain on paper towels.

TO SERVE: Arrange the endive halves on a heated platter, sprinkle with parsley and garnish with the lemon wedges.

GRILLED STEAMED LEEKS

Poireaux Grillés

Serves 6

12 medium leeks
1 cup olive oil
Salt and freshly ground white pepper to taste

Preheat the broiler or prepare the grill.

PREPARING THE LEEKS: Treat leeks with care or they'll ruin your dishes with an unpleasant grittiness. To prepare leeks, first cut the green part off the stalks, then cut each leek in half lengthwise to within 1″ of the root. Fan the leaves apart as you hold the stalk under running water. Be sure to flush all the sand out. Drain off excess water and set aside.

Bring 2 cups of salted water to a boil in a large saucepan over high heat. Add the leeks, cover and steam until the leeks are tender and can be easily pierced with a knife (5–8 minutes). The steaming time will vary according to the size of the leeks. If all the leeks won't fit in a single layer, you can double them up. However, halfway through the steaming you'll have to flip the layers, so the top layer of leeks is now on the bottom.

After the steaming has finished, empty the hot water out of the pan and fill it with cold water to cool the leeks. Grab each leek by the root and give it a final swish in the water to rid it of any remaining sand. Drain all the leeks of excess water, place them in a container and cover them with the olive oil. They'll keep for several days, refrigerated.

When you're ready to serve them, shake off the excess oil, season with salt and pepper and broil under or grill over very high heat, turning occasionally until they blacken nicely on all sides.

Asparagus with Hollandaise Sauce

Asperges, Sauce Hollandaise

Serves 6

3 bunches asparagus (4–6 spears per person)
1½ cups hollandaise sauce (See recipe on page 101.)

There are several schools of thought on how to prepare asparagus. The traditional method is to bend the stalk gently from tip to stem until it breaks naturally. The stem end is usually tough and fibrous and may be discarded. An alternative is to cut a deep peel off the stem end of the stalk (taking it down $^1/_{16}''$ all the way around). This eliminates much of the outer fibrous layer and provides a longer portion of edible stalk. With either method, you can peel the skin off the entire stalk if you prefer. For appearance's sake, cut all the stalks to the same length.

In a sauté pan large enough to hold the asparagus in one layer (use 2 pans, if necessary, or cook the asparagus spears in batches), bring 2″ of salted water to a boil. It's essential to blanch the asparagus spears in a shallow pan so they can't bang around and break apart. Boil the asparagus in a single layer for 3 minutes, or until crisp, but cooked.

TO SERVE: Arrange the asparagus in parallel rows on a warmed serving platter. Ladle a streak of hollandaise across the center of the stalks. Serve the rest of the hollandaise on the side.

Ratatouille

Serves 6

4 medium tomatoes
1 medium red bell pepper
1 medium green pepper
1 small eggplant
1 small zucchini
1 medium onion
¾ cup olive oil
1 tablespoon minced garlic
2 whole bay leaves
2 teaspoons fennel seed
2 teaspoons finely chopped fresh oregano (or 1 teaspoon dried)
2 teaspoons finely chopped fresh basil (or 1 teaspoon dried)
1 cup tomato purée
2 tablespoons sugar
Salt to taste
1 tablespoon freshly ground black pepper
1 cup pitted black olives
½ cup water, or as needed
1 teaspoon red pepper flakes
¼ cup finely chopped parsley

Bring 6 cups of salted water to a boil. Drop the tomatoes into the water for 15 seconds, then plunge them into ice water to stop the cooking and shrivel the skins. When the tomatoes have cooled, their skins will slide off easily. Cut the peeled tomatoes into quarters, squeeze out the seeds and discard the stems. You should have about 2 cups of tomato quarters.

Cut the red and green peppers in half. Remove the membranes, seeds and stems. Dice the halves into 1″ pieces. You should have about 1 cup of each pepper.

Leaving the skin on, dice the eggplant into 1″ cubes. You should have about 1 cup.

Slice the zucchini into rounds ½″ thick. You should have about 1 cup.

Peel and cut the onion into quarters, then cut each quarter once across the grain. You should have about 1 cup of coarsely chopped onions.

Heat the olive oil in a large Dutch oven over medium-high heat. (Traditionally, the *ratatouille* of Provence uses a lot of oil. If you wish, you can use less oil, making a drier dish.) Add the red and green peppers and the onions. Sauté for 2 minutes. Lower the heat to medium if the vegetables begin to burn.

Add all of the remaining ingredients, except the chopped parsley, and cook over medium heat for 15 minutes, stirring occasionally so nothing sticks to the bottom of the pot.

After 15 minutes, add the chopped parsley and cook 5 minutes longer. Serve immediately as a side vegetable, or chill for a great addition to a cold salad plate.

Stuffed Zucchini

Courgettes Farcies

Serves 6

Stuffed zucchini are a great way to use leftover ratatouille. Chilled, they also make an interesting addition to a cold salad plate.

3 zucchini squashes, about 6″ long and 1½″ thick
1 cup ratatouille (See previous recipe.)
¼ cup fresh bread crumbs
½ cup cooked rice
Salt and freshly ground black pepper to taste
¼ cup grated Swiss cheese
¼ cup olive oil

Preheat oven to 400 degrees.

Wash the zucchini in cold water. Cut them in half lengthwise, trim the ends and scoop out the seeds. The prepared zucchini should resemble empty canoes.

Put the zucchini in a steamer over boiling water. Steam them for 1 minute. Plunge them into ice water to stop the cooking, then pat dry.

Chop the ratatouille mixture into a chunky paste and mix it with the bread crumbs and rice. Season with salt and pepper. Fill the zucchini with the mixture, mounding it in the center of each squash. Place the zucchini in an oven-proof casserole, taking care not to crowd them too close together. Sprinkle with the grated cheese and drizzle with the olive oil. Bake for 20 minutes, or until the cheese is golden brown.

BRAISED RED CABBAGE

Chou Rouge Braisé

Serves 8

This is one of my family's holiday favorites, a special treat with roast goose. You can make it the traditional way with goose or duck fat, or, if you prefer, simply use bacon fat or vegetable oil.

¼ cup goose fat, duck fat, bacon fat or vegetable oil
2 cups onions, sliced ¼" thick
2 teaspoons minced garlic
2 cups McIntosh apples, skins left on, sliced ¼" thick
2 pounds red cabbage, shredded or sliced thin (as for cole slaw)
1 cup red wine vinegar
2 cups dry red wine
2 cinnamon sticks
2 small whole bay leaves
⅛ teaspoon ground cloves
1 teaspoon ground ginger
1 cup packed brown sugar
Salt and freshly ground white pepper to taste

Heat the fat or oil in a large Dutch oven over medium-high heat. Add the onions, garlic and apples and sauté them for 5 minutes. Add the shredded cabbage and sauté for 2 more minutes, blending the ingredients together. Add the remaining ingredients, season with salt and pepper and bring to a boil.

Reduce the heat to low, cover the pot and simmer for 1 hour, stirring occasionally so nothing sticks to the bottom of the pan. Add a little water if the mixture begins to stick or seems too dry.

After 1 hour, test the cabbage for doneness. It should be firm, but not crisp. Remove the cinnamon sticks and bay leaves. Use a slotted spoon to transfer the cabbage, onions and apples to a serving dish, leaving the liquid in the Dutch oven.

TO SERVE: Increase the heat under the pot to medium. Reduce the cooking juices until they've thickened slightly, enough to coat the back of a spoon. Pour the reduced juices over the cabbage. Taste the cabbage and adjust the seasoning with salt and pepper. Serve immediately.

BOSTON BAKED BEANS

Serves 8–10

3 cups white pea beans, soaked overnight in 6 cups water
½ cup brown sugar
3 tablespoons molasses
1½ teaspoons salt
1 teaspoon dry mustard
1 teaspoon ground ginger
1 teaspoon Worcestershire sauce
1 pound salt pork with some lean meat attached, diced into ½″
    pieces
1 cup onions, diced into ¼″ pieces

Preheat oven to 250 degrees.

Drain the beans but save the water. In a large mixing bowl, combine the beans with the brown sugar, molasses, salt, mustard, ginger and Worcestershire sauce, blending well. On the bottom of a bean pot or Dutch oven place ¼ pound of the salt pork. Add the onions, then the bean mixture. Cover with half of the reserved water and the remaining salt pork.

Bring the beans to a boil over medium-high heat. Remove from heat and cover the pot with aluminum foil. Transfer the pot to the oven and bake for 6–8 hours, checking every half hour or so to see if the liquid has reduced. Add the reserved water as needed, to keep the beans moist. Serve immediately as a hearty side dish, or refrigerate and serve chilled as a picnic dish.

Spicy Bean Curd

Tofu Épicé

Serves 2

For strict vegetarians, this recipe may be prepared using water or vegetable stock instead of chicken stock. Those wishing to prepare their own vegetable stock will find the ingredients listed directly below. For everyone else, please follow the ingredients list beginning with "Spicy Bean Curd."

VEGETABLE STOCK

¾ cup water
½ cup celery, diced into ½″ pieces
½ cup carrots, diced into ½″ pieces
½ cup onions, diced into ½″ pieces
1 teaspoon finely chopped fresh thyme (or ½ teaspoon dried)
1 bay leaf

SPICY BEAN CURD

1 cup converted rice
1 tablespoon vegetable oil
2 tablespoons shiitake mushrooms, sliced ¼″ thick
2 tablespoons red peppers, diced into ½″ pieces
1 tablespoon minced garlic
2 teaspoons minced ginger
½ cup chicken stock (See recipe on page 31.)
2 teaspoons red chili paste with garlic (available in Oriental food stores)
2 tablespoons ketchup
2 tablespoons soy sauce
1 tablespoon red wine vinegar
1 tablespoon dry sherry
3 tablespoons sugar
1 tablespoon sesame oil
2 tablespoons scallions, cut into ⅛″ pieces
½ cup bamboo shoots, diced into ¼″ pieces
8 ounces firm bean curd, diced into ½″ cubes
1½ tablespoons cornstarch
2 tablespoons water
½ cup mung bean sprouts

MAKING THE VEGETABLE STOCK: Bring the water to a boil over high heat. Add the stock ingredients, reduce the heat to medium and allow the stock to simmer for 20 minutes. Strain and reserve. You should have ½ cup of stock.

MAKING THE RICE: Bring 2 cups of water to a boil in a heavy-bottomed saucepan over high heat. Add the rice, cover the pan and reduce the heat to low. Cook the rice for 20 minutes, then remove the pan from the heat. Let the rice sit, covered, for 10 minutes.

MAKING THE SPICY BEAN CURD: While the rice is cooking, heat the vegetable oil in a large, heavy-bottomed sauté pan or a wok over medium heat. Add the mushrooms, red pepper, garlic and ginger. Sauté, stirring, for 1 minute. Add the chicken stock (or vegetable stock or water) and all the remaining ingredients except the cornstarch, bean sprouts and rice. Bring to a boil, then reduce the heat to medium-low and let simmer for 2 minutes.

Mix the cornstarch with 2 tablespoons of water to form a smooth, runny paste.

Add the cornstarch and sprouts to the bean curd mixture and simmer for 1 minute, or until the liquid in the pan thickens enough to coat the back of a spoon.

TO SERVE: Mound the rice on warmed plates and top with the spicy bean curd mixture.

OVEN-ROASTED CARROTS AND POTATOES

Rôti de Carottes et Pommes de Terre

Serves 6

3 large baking potatoes
6 large carrots
4 tablespoons vegetable oil
Salt and freshly ground black pepper to taste

3 tablespoons finely chopped parsley, for garnish

Preheat oven to 400 degrees.

Peel the potatoes. Cut them in quarters lengthwise, like very thick french fries. Peel the carrots. Cut them in half crosswise and then in half lengthwise.

Place the carrots and potatoes in an oven-proof pan. Add the vegetable oil and salt and pepper. Toss the vegetables until they're evenly coated with oil and seasonings.

Roast uncovered for 45–55 minutes, stirring every 10 minutes, until all the carrots and potatoes are evenly browned.

TO SERVE: Alternate carrots and potatoes on a warmed serving platter. Sprinkle with chopped parsley and serve.

SWISS POTATOES

Pommes de Terre Roesti

Serves 6

1½ pounds russet potatoes
3 tablespoons vegetable oil
2 tablespoons unsalted butter
¼ cup onion, sliced ¼″ thick
1 teaspoon minced garlic
⅛ teaspoon freshly grated nutmeg
Salt and freshly ground white pepper to taste

The night before you intend to serve this dish, boil the potatoes, unpeeled, until they're tender (30–40 minutes). Drain the potatoes and refrigerate overnight.

Peel the potatoes, slice very thin and then chop. Set aside.

Heat the vegetable oil and butter in a 10″ non-stick sauté pan over medium-high heat. Add the onions and garlic and sauté for 2 minutes, then add all the remaining ingredients and blend well.

Press down on the potato mixture with a spatula to form a uniform pancake (about ½″ thick). Cook the potato cake until the underside is golden brown and very crisp, then pull the pan off the heat. Invert a plate on top of the pan and *carefully* flip the pan so the uncooked side of the potatoes is on the dinner plate. Now slide the potatoes back into the pan and brown the uncooked side, once again pressing down on the potatoes with the spatula.

TO SERVE: When the potato pancake is very crisp, slide it out of the pan onto a warmed serving plate. Cut it into wedges and serve immediately.

CHAPTER 9

SALADS

One of my favorite food stories tells of a Mexican restaurateur who memorialized himself with a salad. This particular restaurant needed tourist traffic the way a farm needs rain—too much of a good thing spells disaster. One busload of tourists gave a nice lift to the luncheon business. Two busloads was better, even if the cooks, in their haste to serve so many, tended to undersalt the chicken. But three busloads was a catastrophe. The waiters couldn't possibly keep pace with the jabbering horde of hungry *norteamericanos*. Worst of all, the food ran out.

Such was the position of the restaurateur, whose name, incidentally, was César. The wild-eyed chef grabbed the few ingredients left in the kitchen—a case of eggs, a few crates of romaine lettuce, anchovies that no one had yet put to use, and all the garlic and stale bread scraps he could find. He instructed the waiters to tell the impatient diners that the restaurant was serving only one luncheon entrée, the special house salad (which he was inventing at that very moment).

We know his creation as Caesar Salad.

I love this story, if only because it demonstrates where inventiveness and courage in the kitchen will take you. Salad is the most spontaneous of all culinary undertakings, the most forgiving of a last minute addition or alteration. Just about any vegetable (it needn't be leafy) can be the basis for a salad. Meat, fish and poultry, especially with an interesting vinaigrette or mayonnaise dressing, will expand your salad repertoire as well as provide you with a host of light entrées. I once prepared a salad in my home that had over thirty different ingredients. Unfortunately it took me two hours to assemble.

My family foraged regularly for salad ingredients—dandelion leaves, skunk cabbage and wild watercress. Skunk cabbage, especially the tender young leaves, has a taste that resembles Chinese bok choy, and dandelion leaves, with their peppery flavor, offer a poor-man's alternative to arugula and radicchio, practically unknown in the New York of my childhood. Radicchio, a type of red-leaf chicory from Italy, the *dernier cri* in the world of stylish salad greens, used to wander no further afield than the kitchens of Trentino cooks, who not only served it in conventional cold salads, but were grilling it with olive oil, black pepper and fennel long before grilled salads became the watchword of the mesquite set. I like to use it as a garnish, not just because it has a distinctive flavor, but because the vibrant purple leaves add an attractive contrast to paler ingredients.

Seasonal restrictions no longer hamper the devoted fan of green salads the way they once did. Romaine lettuce, radicchio, arugula and red leaf lettuce are available on a year-round basis—although I'll start to believe in miracles only when a produce wholesaler comes to me in January with a tomato to match the fat red orbs that come out of a New England garden in July. Some seasonal rhythms will always prevail. But your imagination—and salad's sheer versatility—will always supply you with ingredients for a delicious combination.

CAESAR SALAD

Salade César

Serves 4

1 head romaine lettuce
¼ cup + 3 tablespoons olive oil
1 cup French bread cubes (½″ cubes)
2 cloves garlic, peeled
12 anchovies (approximately 2-ounce tin)
2 teaspoons Worcestershire sauce
2 teaspoons dry mustard
1½ tablespoons lemon juice
2 teaspoons freshly ground black pepper
3 egg yolks, from large eggs, at room temperature
½ cup grated Parmesan cheese
Salt to taste

Cut the lettuce across the head into slices 1″ thick. Discard the core and rinse the slices in cold water. Drain the lettuce, pat it dry, wrap it in a tea towel and refrigerate for 30 minutes to crisp the leaves.

To make croutons, heat the ¼ cup of olive oil in a sauté pan over medium-high heat. Fry the bread cubes in the oil, tossing frequently, until they're crisp and golden. Drain the croutons on a paper towel.

Put the garlic cloves in a large wooden salad bowl. Mash the cloves against the sides of the bowl with the back of a wooden spoon. Rub the pieces against the bowl until they begin to disintegrate. Remove the pieces and discard. Oil from the garlic will remain in the bowl and flavor the salad.

Add the anchovies and repeat the procedure you used with the garlic, but leave the anchovy pieces in the bowl.

Now add the 3 tablespoons of olive oil, the Worcestershire sauce, dry mustard, lemon juice, black pepper and egg yolks and blend well. Add the lettuce, croutons, Parmesan cheese and season with salt. Toss everything together and serve directly from the salad bowl.

LEAF LETTUCE WITH TRUFFLE DRESSING

Salade de Laitue, Mélange aux Truffes

Serves 6

Each batch of balsamic vinegar gets its distinctive flavor from its "mother," the bacterial must lining the vinegar casks. Distinguished *balsamici*, made from musts passed like heirlooms from one generation of an Italian family to its offspring, are often part of a bride's dowry.

SALAD

1 head red leaf lettuce
1 head radicchio lettuce
1 head Boston or Bibb lettuce

TRUFFLE DRESSING

Yields about 1¼ cups

¼ cup balsamic vinegar
3 tablespoons red wine vinegar
¼ cup walnut oil
½ cup vegetable oil
¼ teaspoon minced garlic
1 teaspoon black truffle, finely chopped
2 tablespoons truffle juice (liquid from the can or jar in which the truffle was packed)
Salt and freshly ground white pepper to taste

6 sprigs of a fresh herb (such as thyme, rosemary, sage), for garnish

Separate the lettuce leaves from the cores and wash them well. Drain the leaves, pat dry and wrap in a tea towel. Refrigerate the bundle for 30 minutes to crisp the leaves.

To make the vinaigrette, place all of the ingredients in a bowl and mix together with a whisk.

Tear the lettuce leaves into bite-size pieces and place them in a large salad bowl. Add the truffle dressing and toss everything well. You may add more or less dressing as you prefer. Divide the salad among 6 salad plates, garnishing each with 1 sprig of fresh herb.

Lobster Salad

Salade de Homard

Serves 4

1½ pounds cooked lobster meat (available at seafood markets), cut
    into 1″ pieces
⅔ cup mayonnaise (See recipe on page 105.)
3 tablespoons celery, diced into ¼″ pieces
Salt and freshly ground white pepper to taste
1 head Boston or Bibb lettuce

GARNISH

4 lemon wedges
2 hard-boiled eggs, each cut into 4 wedges
2 tomatoes, each cut into 4 wedges
4 teaspoons capers, drained

Place the lobster meat, mayonnaise and celery in a bowl and season with salt and pepper. Mix the ingredients together well, cover the bowl with plastic wrap and refrigerate the salad until it is to be served.

Separate the lettuce leaves from the core and wash them well. You'll need 8 good-sized leaves. Drain the leaves, pat dry and wrap in a tea towel. Refrigerate the bundle for 30 minutes to crisp the leaves.

TO SERVE: Place 2 lettuce leaves on each of 4 chilled plates. Mound the lobster mixture atop the leaves. Garnish each plate with 1 lemon wedge, 2 wedges of hard-boiled egg, 2 tomato wedges and 1 teaspoon of capers.

SALAD NANON

Salade Nanon

Serves 6

3 heads Boston or Bibb lettuce
6 hard-boiled eggs
½ cup walnuts, coarsely chopped
1 cup mustard vinaigrette (See recipe below.)

Separate the lettuce leaves from the cores and wash them well. Drain the leaves, pat dry and wrap in a tea towel. Refrigerate the bundle for 30 minutes to crisp the leaves.

Slice the eggs into ⅛″ slices—an egg-slicer makes this very easy.

TO SERVE: Arrange the lettuce leaves on 6 chilled salad plates. Place the egg slices decoratively on the lettuce and sprinkle the salad with the walnuts. Drizzle 2 tablespoons or so of mustard vinaigrette over each salad.

MUSTARD VINAIGRETTE

Vinaigrette à la Moutarde

Yields about 1½ cups

¼ cup white distilled vinegar
1 tablespoon sherry wine vinegar
1 tablespoon Dijon mustard
½ teaspoon anchovy, minced
¼ teaspoon Worcestershire sauce
⅛ teaspoon Tabasco sauce
¼ teaspoon minced garlic
Salt and freshly ground white pepper to taste
1 tablespoon walnut oil
1 cup olive oil

Combine all of the ingredients, except the olive oil, in the bowl of a food processor. Blend for 1 minute and then, with the machine on, slowly add the olive oil in a thin steady stream.

RITZ-CARLTON CAFE SALAD

Salade Ritz-Carlton Cafe

Serves 8

1 log Montrachet goat cheese (10 ounces)
8 sprigs of a fresh herb (such as thyme, rosemary, sage)
1 tablespoon freshly ground black pepper
2 cups olive oil
2 heads Boston or Bibb lettuce
1 head radicchio lettuce
4 heads Belgian endive
8 sprigs rosemary
8 cherry tomatoes, cut into quarters
1 cup mustard vinaigrette (See previous recipe.)

Cut the goat cheese into 16 rounds and place them in a container that will hold them in 1 layer. Distribute the herb sprigs evenly over the cheese and sprinkle with 1 tablespoon of black pepper. Pour the olive oil over the rounds so that oil covers them completely. If it doesn't, add more olive oil. Cover the container with plastic wrap and refrigerate overnight.

Separate the lettuce, radicchio and endive leaves from the cores and wash them. Drain the lettuce and endive and pat dry. Wrap in tea towels and refrigerate for 30 minutes to crisp.

Set aside 24 spears of endive. Cut the remaining endive into ¼" slices and set aside.

ASSEMBLING THE SALAD: Place 3 spears of endive on each of 8 chilled salad plates in the 10, 12 and 2 o'clock positions. Drape 2 leaves of lettuce over the endive spears, leaving 1" of the endive tips exposed. Mound the sliced endive atop the lettuce. Place a sprig of rosemary on one side of the plate and 1 quartered cherry tomato on the other.

Place a leaf of radicchio at the bottom of the plate. Set 2 rounds of goat cheese atop the radicchio leaf. (Save the olive oil in which the cheese marinated. Use it in salad dressing, for flavoring stews or for sautéing meats or fish.) Drizzle 2 tablespoons of mustard vinaigrette over the salad.

VEGETABLE AND MUSHROOM SALAD

Salade aux Légumes et Champignons

Serves 6

SALAD

2 heads Boston or Bibb lettuce
1 cup broccoli flowerets, cut into ½″ pieces
1 cup cauliflower flowerets, cut into ½″ pieces
1 cup green beans, cut into 1″ pieces
1 cup asparagus, cut into 1″ pieces
½ cup carrots, cut into julienne strips ⅛″ x 2″
½ cup red peppers, diced into ½″ pieces
1 cup Belgian endive, cut into ½″ pieces
1 cup white mushrooms, sliced ¼″ thick
1 cup shiitake mushrooms, sliced ¼″ thick

VINAIGRETTE

Yields about 1¼ cups

½ cup balsamic vinegar
2 teaspoons minced garlic
1 teaspoon fresh tarragon, finely chopped (or ½ teaspoon dried)
2 teaspoons freshly ground black pepper
½ cup safflower oil
Salt to taste

Separate the lettuce leaves from the cores and wash them well. Drain the leaves, pat dry and wrap in a tea towel. Refrigerate the bundle for 30 minutes to crisp the leaves.

Bring a large pot of salted water to boil over high heat. You will use this water to blanch some of the vegetables. Do not allow the vegetables to cook so long that they lose their crispness.

Add the broccoli to the boiling water and cook for 3–4 minutes. Immediately remove the flowerets with a slotted spoon and plunge them into a bath of ice water to stop the cooking.

Add the cauliflower to the boiling water, cooking 3–4 minutes. Immediately remove them with a slotted spoon and plunge them into the ice water with the broccoli.

Repeat the procedure with the green beans, asparagus, carrots—cooking each in turn for 2–3 minutes and adding them to the bath of ice water.

Drain and pat dry all of the blanched vegetables and place them in a large bowl. Add the red peppers, endive and both kinds of mushrooms to the bowl.

MAKING THE VINAIGRETTE: Combine the vinegar, garlic, tarragon and pepper in a small bowl. Slowly add the oil in a steady stream while whisking the vinaigrette with a wire whip. Season with salt.

TO SERVE: Add the vinaigrette to the bowl of vegetables and toss everything well. Line each of 6 chilled salad plates with lettuce leaves. Place a mound of dressed vegetables in the center of each plate.

WATERCRESS AND RADISH SALAD

Salade de Cresson et Radis

Serves 4

This salad is a nice example of the way the dominant characteristic of one ingredient (in this case, the peppery flavor of watercress) emphasizes the same quality in a second ingredient (radishes). The zip of the vegetables would overpower an ordinary vinaigrette, so I use balsamic vinegar in this dressing.

1 bunch watercress
2 tablespoons safflower oil
2 tablespoons balsamic vinegar
2 teaspoons freshly ground black pepper
Salt to taste
1 cup radishes, cut into quarters

Pick the watercress of stems and wash it well. Drain, pat dry and wrap it in a tea towel. Refrigerate the bundle for 30 minutes to crisp the leaves.

Combine the safflower oil, balsamic vinegar and pepper in a bowl and season with salt.

TO SERVE: Add the watercress to the bowl with the vinaigrette and toss everything well. Drain the watercress of any excess dressing. On each of 4 chilled salad plates, form the watercress into nests. Toss the radish quarters in the bowl with the remaining vinaigrette. Drain the radishes of excess dressing and mound them in the center of the watercress nests.

SHRIMP ORIENTAL

Salade Orientale aux Crevettes

Serves 4

SHRIMP

4 cups fish stock (recipe on page 32) or water
½ cup celery, diced into ½″ pieces
½ cup onions, diced into ½″ pieces
2 bay leaves, crumbled
4 whole cloves
1 teaspoon cayenne pepper
36 large shrimp

SALAD

24 snow peas
1 head radicchio lettuce
½ cup red peppers, diced into ½″ pieces
½ cup green peppers, diced into ½″ pieces
½ cup mandarin orange sections
¼ cup scallions, sliced on the bias into 1″ pieces
1 cup whole canned water chestnuts
1 teaspoon minced garlic
1 tablespoon finely chopped fresh ginger
¼ cup soy sauce
¼ cup sesame oil
Salt and freshly ground black pepper to taste

1 cup alfalfa sprouts, for garnish

COOKING THE SHRIMP: Bring the fish stock or water, celery, onions, bay leaves, cloves and cayenne pepper to a boil in a large saucepan over high heat. Reduce the heat to medium and simmer for 3 minutes. Add the shrimp. Once the water begins to simmer, cook for another 4 minutes. Drain and cool the shrimp. When cool, peel, devein and chill.

PREPARING THE VEGETABLES: Bring 4 cups of salted water to a boil in a saucepan over high heat. Add the snow peas and cook for 1–2 minutes. They should remain bright green and crisp. Tip the snow peas into a colander and rinse under cold running water to stop the cooking. Pat dry. Wrap in a tea towel and chill.

Separate the lettuce leaves from the core and wash them well. You will need 8 leaves. Drain the leaves, pat dry and wrap in a tea towel. Refrigerate the bundle for 30 minutes to crisp the leaves.

TO SERVE: Combine the cooked shrimp and all of the salad ingredients, except the lettuce, in a large mixing bowl and toss well. Allow the mixture to marinate at room temperature for 15 minutes. Place 2 overlapping radicchio leaves at the top of each plate and spread ¼ cup alfalfa sprouts over the bottom of the plate. Mound equal portions of the salad on each plate.

GRILLED CHICKEN AND GOAT CHEESE SALAD

Salade de Poulet Grillé et Fromage de Chèvre

Serves 4

This salad is best if made twenty-four hours in advance.

1 log Montrachet goat cheese (10 ounces)
8 sprigs of a fresh herb (e.g., thyme, rosemary, sage)
1 tablespoon freshly ground black pepper
2¾ cups olive oil
1 large red pepper, diced into ½" pieces
1 large green pepper, diced into ½" pieces
1 cup white mushrooms, sliced ¼" thick
½ teaspoon finely chopped fresh basil (or ¼ teaspoon dried)
1 teaspoon finely chopped fresh thyme (or ½ teaspoon dried)
½ teaspoon finely chopped fresh rosemary (or ¼ teaspoon dried)
¼ cup dry white wine
2 cups Belgian endive, cut into ½" pieces
¼ cup red wine vinegar
Salt and freshly ground black pepper to taste
8 half-breasts of chicken, boneless, skin on, approximately
    4 ounces each
1 head Boston or Bibb lettuce

8 cherry tomatoes, for garnish
4 sprigs watercress, for garnish

Cut the goat cheese into 8 rounds. Place the rounds in a container that will hold them in 1 layer. Distribute the herb sprigs evenly over the cheese and sprinkle with the black pepper. Pour 2 cups of olive oil over the rounds. They should be completely covered by the oil. If not, add more oil. Cover the container with plastic wrap and refrigerate overnight.

Heat 2 tablespoons olive oil in a large sauté pan over medium-high heat. Add the peppers and mushrooms and sauté, stirring constantly, for 2–3 minutes. Add the chopped herbs and wine. Increase the heat to high and bring the mixture to a boil. Cook for 2 minutes. Remove the pan from the heat, add the endive, ½ cup of olive oil and the red wine vinegar. Season with salt and pepper. Put the vegetable mixture into a bowl and cover with plastic wrap. Refrigerate overnight.

Preheat the broiler or prepare the grill.

Brush the chicken breasts with 2 tablespoons of olive oil and season with salt and pepper. Broil or grill using high heat until done (10–12 minutes). Allow them to cool, then chill them in the refrigerator.

Separate the lettuce leaves from the core and rinse under cold running water. Drain, pat dry and wrap in a tea towel. Refrigerate the bundle for 30 minutes to crisp.

When you are ready to serve the salad, cut each chicken breast into 4 diagonal slices.

TO SERVE: Place 2 lettuce leaves in the center of each of 4 chilled plates. Mound ½ cup of the vegetable mixture atop the lettuce. Fan a sliced chicken breast to the left of the vegetables; fan a second breast to the right. Place 2 goat cheese rounds at the bottom of the plate. (Save the olive oil in which the cheese marinated. Use it in salad dressing, for flavoring stews or for sautéing meats or fish.) Garnish each plate with 2 cherry tomatoes and a sprig of watercress.

CHICKEN SALAD À LA RITZ-CARLTON

Salade de Poulet à la Ritz-Carlton

Serves 4

2 large chicken breasts, bone in, skin on, approximately 1 pound each
1 head Boston or Bibb lettuce
⅔ cup mayonnaise (See recipe on page 105.)
3 tablespoons celery, diced into ¼″ pieces
Salt and freshly ground white pepper to taste

GARNISH

1 avocado, peeled, cut into 8 wedges
8 radishes, cut into quarters
4 teaspoons capers

Bring a large pot of salted water to a boil over high heat, add the chicken breasts and reduce the heat to medium-low. Simmer until the chicken is done (about 20 minutes). Remove the chicken from the water and allow to cool. Chill in the refrigerator. Save the cooking liquid for soup or broth.

Separate the lettuce leaves from the core and wash them well. You'll need 8 good-sized leaves. Drain, pat dry and wrap in a tea towel. Refrigerate the bundle for 30 minutes to crisp the leaves.

Remove the skin and bone from the chilled chicken breasts and cut the meat into 1″ pieces. Mix it in a bowl with the mayonnaise and celery. Season with salt and pepper.

TO SERVE: Line each of 4 chilled salad plates with 2 lettuce leaves. Mound the chicken salad in the center of each plate. Garnish with 2 avocado wedges, 8 radish quarters and 1 teaspoon of capers.

CHAPTER 10

SAVORIES

When English investors wanted to open a first-class hotel in London, later to be known as the Savoy, they selected César Ritz and Auguste Escoffier, premier *hôtelier* and master chef, to do the job. Escoffier soon discovered that the voracious English diners expected heartier preludes to dessert than the salad and sorbet that contemporary French cuisine then typically offered. To his horror, the English loved capping off an exquisitely prepared entrée with something as mundane as toast smothered in melted cheese or creamed mushrooms. The use of savories, Escoffier pronounced in his *Guide Culinaire*, "opposed gastronomic principles." There was no reason any good menu ought to feature them.

Strong language. I should note that his personal feelings notwithstanding, the master yielded to the English demand for savories after a main course. In his chapter devoted to savories and hors-d'oeuvres he quickly has his say, then resignedly promises not to preach to the reader. He provides dozens of recipes devoted to this most English of all food courses, including familiar British standbys like Welsh rarebit, angels on horseback and Scotch woodcock.

What, exactly, is a savory? How can you tell one from an hors-d'oeuvre? The answer lies primarily in the circumstances in which it's served. Imagine a rotund Victorian trencherman—remember, stoutness was then a sign of health—boldly thrashing through smoked salmon and goose terrine in aspic, gurgling down a soup course of unbridled richness, say, cream of mussels and saffron, all this before embarking on the serious business of the meal—rack of venison with black peppercorns. Naturally, having polished off the venison, he slows down a bit, but . . . there's a small gap between the entrée and sweet (cheese, nuts and port will appear in due turn, after the dessert). Into this gap, this chink of eating space, goes—you guessed it—the savory.

Savories seem rougher hewn, less expressive of finesse, than the endless French concoctions which used to parade across the tables of England's great houses or fine restaurants. Humble toast points, fashioned from ordinary white bread, ballast hundreds of savory recipes that depend on eggs or creamed something-or-other, most likely seasoned with cayenne pepper. If this sounds reminiscent of impromtu Sunday fare or an informal hors-d'oeuvre, it's because the identical dish often accompanies afternoon tea or fills the stomach of the British insomniac—functions that make much more sense than savories' exalted status during the Victorian and Edwardian eras.

When The Ritz-Carlton, Boston opened in 1927, English chefs were still trundling out savories after the main course, a practice never adopted by the Boston hotel. Over the years, our kitchen has used these small, charmingly informal dishes as late night snacks or, in the years preceding the war, as part of the menu for The Rooftop Garden, a club that treated Bostonians to equal servings of light food and swing music. Today, the hungry late-arriving guest and the couple in search of an after-theater supper have their pick of a half-dozen savories in The Cafe. Eggs, cheese, toast, maybe some anchovies or mustard for a bit of spice—a few of our recipes are hallowed Ritz-Carlton (and Escoffier) favorites. My special challenge is to expand on that special culinary terrain that falls somewhere between appetizers and entrées. Whether we've succeeded, with dishes like lobster and corn stew, cheddar cheese bread pudding, and deep-fried camembert, is a decision you'll have to make.

WELSH RAREBIT

Serves 6

1¼ pounds sharp Wisconsin or New York cheddar cheese,
  shredded
½ pound Colby cheese, shredded
½ pound yellow American cheese, shredded
1 cup light cream
2 cups heavy cream
½ cup strong dark ale
1 tablespoon Worcestershire sauce
⅛ teaspoon cayenne pepper
2 teaspoons dry mustard
6 small tomatoes
3–4 tablespoons olive oil
Freshly ground black pepper to taste
12 slices hearty, homemade-style white bread, trimmed of crusts,
  toasted and cut in half diagonally

Preheat the broiler.

Melt the cheese in the top of a double boiler over medium heat. The water should be simmering, not boiling rapidly.

While the cheese is melting, combine the light and heavy cream and the ale in a saucepan and bring to a boil over high heat. As soon as the mixture boils, remove the saucepan from the heat and cover to keep warm.

When the cheese has melted, slowly add the cream mixture, stirring constantly until it's well-blended. Add the Worcestershire sauce, cayenne pepper and mustard and blend well. Rarebit should be thick but still pourable. Adjust the consistency with more ale or cream, if necessary.

Cut the stems off the tomatoes. Slice the tomatoes in half. Smear the halves with olive oil and sprinkle with black pepper. Place under a hot broiler and cook until they soften (about 3–5 minutes).

TO SERVE: Place 2 tomato halves on each of 6 plates. Arrange 4 toast points around the tomatoes and pour 1 cup of hot rarebit over each plate.

ANGELS ON HORSEBACK

Serves 4

6 slices white bread
1 cup dry bread crumbs
½ teaspoon cayenne pepper
24 large oysters, shucked
12 slices bacon

4 sprigs parsley, for garnish
4 lemon wedges, for garnish

Preheat the broiler.

Cut 4 rounds, 1½″ in diameter, out of each slice of bread. Toast the rounds and reserve.

Mix the bread crumbs with the cayenne pepper in a bowl. Toss the oysters, 6 at a time, in the bread crumbs to coat them evenly. Cut the bacon slices in half. Roll each oyster in a slice of bacon and fasten with a toothpick.

Broil the oysters for 5–7 minutes, turning them once, until they're brown and crisp on all sides. Pour off the juice as it accumulates in the broiling pan or the oysters will become soggy.

TO SERVE: Remove the toothpicks and place an oyster on each toast round. Use frilled decorative toothpicks to skewer the oysters to the toast rounds. Place on a serving platter and garnish with parsley and lemon wedges.

SCOTCH WOODCOCK

Serves 4

8 large eggs
½ cup light cream
½ teaspoon salt
⅛ teaspoon cayenne pepper
2 tablespoons unsalted butter
12 anchovies (approximately 2-ounce tin), drained

1 tablespoon chives, cut into 1″ lengths, for garnish

Combine the eggs, light cream, salt and cayenne pepper in a mixing bowl and beat until well-mixed. Melt the butter in a large non-stick sauté pan over medium heat. Add the eggs and scramble them, stirring constantly. Transfer the eggs to a warm serving dish. Crisscross with anchovies and sprinkle with fresh chives to garnish.

CROQUE-MONSIEUR

Serves 6

4 tablespoons Dijon mustard
12 slices hearty, homemade-style white bread, trimmed of crusts
12 thin slices of boiled or Danish-style ham, 1 ounce each
6 thin slices Gruyère cheese, 1 ounce each
6 tablespoons unsalted butter

6 sprigs fresh watercress, for garnish

Spread a light coating of mustard on 1 side of the bread slices. Prepare 6 sandwiches, each containing 2 ounces of ham and 1 ounce of Gruyère cheese.

Melt the butter in a sauté pan over medium heat and cook the sandwiches, 1 or 2 at a time, until golden brown.

TO SERVE: Cut the sandwiches in quarters and arrange them on a serving dish. Garnish with sprigs of watercress.

Steak Tartare en Brochette

Serves 4

3 tablespoons olive oil
1 pound extra-lean ground beef, tenderloin or sirloin
1 tablespoon capers, coarsely chopped
4 anchovies, minced
1 tablespoon minced onions
1 tablespoon finely chopped parsley
2 egg yolks, from large eggs
½ teaspoon cayenne pepper
2 teaspoons Worcestershire sauce
2 teaspoons Dijon mustard
Salt and freshly ground black pepper to taste

4 sprigs parsley, for garnish

Soak 8 bamboo skewers (6″ long) in cold water for 1 hour.

Preheat the broiler.

Coat a broiling pan with 2 tablespoons of olive oil. Combine all of the other ingredients, including the remaining tablespoon of olive oil, in a bowl and mix well. Divide the mixture into 8 portions. Mold each portion into a sausage shape around a skewer. Place the skewers on the greased broiler pan and broil 3 minutes (for medium rare). Transfer the brochettes to a serving platter and garnish with parsley sprigs.

CHEDDAR CHEESE BREAD PUDDING

Serves 6

6 tablespoons unsalted butter
6 slices hearty, homemade-style white bread, trimmed of crusts
1½ cups milk
3 large eggs
1 teaspoon salt
⅛ teaspoon Tabasco sauce
1 pound aged sharp cheddar cheese, shredded

Butter a 1½-quart soufflé dish with 1 tablespoon butter. Butter one side of the bread slices with the remaining butter. Cut each slice into thirds.

Beat the milk, eggs, salt and Tabasco sauce together in a mixing bowl.

Arrange half of the bread, buttered side up, on the bottom of the dish. Sprinkle evenly with half of the cheddar, top with the remaining bread, then with the rest of the cheddar. Pour the egg mixture over the bread and cheese. Let stand in the refrigerator for 45 minutes.

Preheat oven to 350 degrees.

Bake until bubbling and golden (40–45 minutes).

TO SERVE: Transfer the hot pudding immediately to the table and serve directly from the soufflé dish.

LOBSTER AND CORN STEW

Serves 4

3 tablespoons + 4 teaspoons unsalted butter
½ pound cooked lobster meat (available at seafood markets), cut
　into 1″ pieces
½ cup corn kernels, fresh or frozen
1 tablespoon paprika
½ cup dry sherry
2 cups light cream
2 cups heavy cream
Salt and freshly ground white pepper to taste
2 tablespoons finely chopped parsley

Melt 3 tablespoons butter in a large saucepan over medium-high heat. Add the lobster, corn and paprika. Sauté, stirring constantly, for 2 minutes. Remove the pan from the heat and add the sherry. Lower the heat to medium and return the pan to the heat. Reduce the sherry by half. Add the cream, salt and pepper. Continue cooking until the cream is completely heated through. Stir in the parsley.

TO SERVE: Ladle the stew into hot bowls and dot with a teaspoon of butter.

FLUFFED EGGS WITH PERRIER, CHIVES AND FOIE GRAS

Serves 1

Fluffing eggs requires intense heat. Consequently, more than three eggs (one portion) cools the pan down too much, scrambling the eggs rather than fluffing them. To make this dish for more than one person, multiply all the ingredients by the number of servings, but only cook one portion in the sauté pan at a time.

¼ cup unsalted butter
3 large eggs
2 tablespoons Perrier water
½ teaspoon chives, cut into ¼″ lengths
Salt and freshly ground white pepper to taste
½ ounce high quality *foie gras*

2 cherry tomatoes, cut in half, for garnish

Preheat the broiler.

Clarify the butter by melting it in a small pan over low heat. Skim the froth of casein that rises to the surface, then spoon out the clear yellow liquid (clarified butter) without disturbing the layer of whey in the bottom of the pan. Save 2 tablespoons of clarified butter for this recipe. Refrigerate any extra for future use.

Beat the eggs with the Perrier and chives. Season with salt and pepper.

Place the foie gras under a broiler until it's heated all the way through and just starting to melt (about 1 minute). While the foie gras is cooking, fluff the eggs.

Heat a 7″ non-stick omelette pan with the clarified butter over high heat until smoking.

Add the eggs. They should immediately "fluff" up the sides of the pan. Shake the pan back and forth while stirring quickly with a heat-resistant, rubber spatula. The eggs should cook in about 15 seconds, fluffing up and doubling in volume, but remain soft. Slide the omelette, unfolded, onto a plate.

TO SERVE: Place the foie gras in the center of the eggs. Garnish with cherry tomato halves.

Fried Oysters on Sauce Verte

Serves 6

24 large oysters on the halfshell
1 cup fresh bread crumbs
2–4 cups vegetable oil
2 cups *sauce verte* (See recipe on page 94.)
2 ounces beluga caviar

24 sprigs fresh dill, for garnish

Remove the oysters from the shells and set the shells aside. Toss the oysters in the bread crumbs, 6 at a time. Refrigerate 30 minutes to set the coating, but don't chill for a longer period or the crumbs will become soggy.

Heat 2 cups of vegetable oil in a small sauté pan or 4 cups in a large sauté pan. If you're using the smaller pan, you'll have to cook the oysters in 2 batches. Heat the oil over medium-high heat until a fat-frying thermometer inserted in the oil reads 375 degrees. Fry the oysters until golden brown (about 3–4 minutes). Drain on paper towels.

TO SERVE: Place 1 tablespoon of sauce verte in each shell and replace the oysters. Put a small knifepoint of caviar atop each oyster and garnish with a sprig of dill.

Cream Puff Pastry

Pâte à Choux

Yields 12 medium cream puffs

1 stick unsalted butter
1 cup water
¼ teaspoon salt
1 cup flour
4 large eggs

Cut the butter into tablespoons. Combine it with the water and salt and bring it to a boil in a large, heavy-bottomed saucepan over high heat. As soon as the butter has melted, remove the pan from the heat and add all the flour.

Reduce the heat to low. Return the pan to the heat. Beat the mixture vigorously with a wooden spoon until it forms a thick mass of dough. As you continue to cook the dough, wisps of steam will rise off its surface. Continue cooking over low heat until the dough ceases to steam and beads of butter appear on its surface. Remove the pan from the heat and allow the mixture to cool for 5 minutes.

Add the eggs, one at a time, completely incorporating each egg before adding the next.

The dough is now ready for combining with other ingredients (such as cheese and seasonings, as in the recipe for three-cheese puffs). You can put the *pâte à choux* in its present form directly into a pastry bag and pipe out shapes for cream puffs and eclairs. Bake them on an ungreased cookie sheet at 400 degrees until golden brown (15–30 minutes, depending on the size of your pastries). *Choux* (cream puffs) should be firm when removed from the oven or they'll collapse and become soggy.

THREE-CHEESE PUFFS

Serves 6

1 recipe *pâte à choux* (See previous recipe.)
¼ cup grated Parmesan cheese
¼ cup finely shredded cheddar cheese
¼ cup finely shredded Gruyère cheese
½ teaspoon salt
½ teaspoon freshly ground white pepper
½ teaspoon cayenne pepper
½ teaspoon dry mustard
½ teaspoon freshly grated nutmeg
1 large egg
1 tablespoon water

Preheat oven to 400 degrees.

Fold the cheeses and seasonings into the pâte à choux. Place the mixture in a pastry bag with a plain tip. Pipe the dough in 1″ balls onto an ungreased baking sheet. Don't crowd them. If you don't have a pastry bag, use a spoon to form the dough balls.

Beat the egg with the water. Brush the cheese balls lightly with the egg wash. Bake for 15 minues or until golden puffed and firm. Be careful—if you remove them from the oven too soon, they'll collapse. Serve while hot.

Scalloped Oysters

Serves 6

1 tablespoon unsalted butter
2 pints shucked oysters in their own liquor
2 cups heavy cream
2 cups coarsely ground saltine cracker crumbs
2 teaspoons freshly grated nutmeg
2 teaspoons freshly ground white pepper

Preheat oven to 350 degrees.

Butter an 8″ x 8″ x 2″ casserole dish.

Strain the oysters and save the liquor.

Blend the oyster liquor and the cream.

Cover the bottom of the casserole dish with ½ cup of crumbs. Arrange a layer of oysters and sprinkle with nutmeg and pepper. Repeat, using all the oysters. (You should get 3 layers.) Finish with a layer of crumbs. Pour the cream mixture over the layered crumbs and oysters.

Bake in the center of the oven until the cream mixture thickens, the casserole begins to bubble and the top browns (about 40 minutes). Serve immediately.

GRILLED STEAMED LEEKS
page 110

ASPARAGUS
page 111

CAESAR SALAD *page 121*

RITZ-CARLTON CAFE SALAD
page 125

SHRIMP ORIENTAL
page 128

DEEP-FRIED CAMEMBERT ON STRAWBERRY FONDUE

Serves 2

STRAWBERRY FONDUE

1 pint strawberries
2 tablespoons sugar
2 tablespoons lemon juice
¼ cup light cream

CHEESE

2 ¼-pound wheels of ripe Camembert cheese
2 large eggs
1 cup fresh bread crumbs
2–4 cups vegetable oil

8 mint leaves, for garnish

MAKING THE FONDUE: Wash and hull the strawberries and purée them in a blender with the sugar, lemon juice and cream. Refrigerate until ready to use.

PREPARING THE CHEESE: Cut each wheel of Camembert into 4 wedges. Whip the eggs. Dip the wedges into the beaten eggs, and then coat them with the bread crumbs. Refrigerate 30 minutes to set the coating and chill the cheese.

Heat 2 cups of vegetable oil in a small sauté pan or 4 cups in a large sauté pan. If you're using the smaller pan, you'll have to cook the cheese in 2 batches. Heat the oil over medium-high heat until a fat-frying thermometer inserted in the oil reads 385 degrees. Fry the cheese wedges until golden brown (about 3–4 minutes). Drain on paper towels.

TO SERVE: Pour a small pool of strawberry fondue on each plate. Place 4 wedges of cheese atop each pool of fondue. Garnish with fresh mint.

Baked Brie en Croûte

Serves 6

½ pound puff pastry (available in 1-pound packages at grocery
    stores)
1 1-pound wheel of ripe Brie cheese
1 large egg
1 tablespoon water
2 Granny Smith apples
18 large strawberries
Juice of ½ lemon

Roll the puff pastry into a sheet ⅛″ thick.

Measure the diameter of the Brie wheel. Cut a circle 6″ larger in diameter out of the sheet of puff pastry. Use the remaining dough to make small decorative shapes—animals, flowers or stars.

Place the Brie in the center of the pastry circle.

Whip the egg with the water and brush a 1″ edge around the pastry circle with the egg wash. Fold the pastry over the cheese to enclose it. Trim off any excess pastry. Turn the enclosed cheese over and brush the top with egg wash. Attach the decorative cut-outs and brush them with egg wash as well. Place the cheese on an ungreased cookie sheet.

Refrigerate for at least 1 hour before baking.

Preheat oven to 400 degrees.

Bake until the pastry rises and turns flaky and golden brown (about 15 minutes).

While the Brie is baking, prepare the fruit. Hull and wash the strawberries. Core the apples and cut into slices ¼″ thick. Put the fruit in a bowl and cover with cold water. Add the lemon juice to prevent the fruit from discoloring.

Let the Brie rest 10 minutes after baking. The cheese should be warm and soft when you cut into it, but not runny.

TO SERVE: Cut the Brie into 6 wedges. Place 1 wedge on each plate. Place a cluster of 3 strawberries to 1 side of each wedge. Arrange a fan of apple slices on the opposite side.

CHAPTER 11

DESSERTS

Why do we so love desserts? Why are desserts the part of the menu that we so often associate with vice—or love? Everyone knows the story of Peach Melba: that Escoffier supposedly invented the dessert for the Australian singer Dame Nellie Melba, for a dinner given in her honor when he was chef at the London Savoy. So far so good. But the authoritative *Larousse Gastronomique* states that Escoffier changed the original dish—an ice swan, holding peaches on its wings, the whole affair resting atop a bed of vanilla ice cream—to peaches with raspberry syrup. Perhaps Gallic tact in the face of unrequited love prevented the *Larousse* from recounting the rumor that Escoffier was infatuated with the opera singer, and when she rejected his advances he changed the dessert to mirror the blood flowing from his broken heart.

Sometimes desserts move beyond the simple desire to repeat an old pleasure or explore a new sweet. On one occasion a Ritz-Carlton patron commissioned a giant cake for his young daughter, who had arrived at the hotel that morning, having recently undergone eye surgery. The girl's first sight, after the removal of her bandages, was an enormous layer cake of yellow génoise (French sponge cake), strawberries and orange butter cream. The cake was crowned with real nasturtiums, glazed strawberries and candied violets. The girl squealed with delight and clapped her hands.

My own German grandmother, in her own way as dedicated as Escoffier, used to spend the entire afternoon making apple strudel for our family. She would work in the dining room, the table covered with a linen cloth for the occasion, rolling out the dough until it was so thin I could see through it. She brushed the dough with a bundle of goose feathers dipped in melted butter. Then, taking care not to rupture the tissue of pastry, she added a layer of apples, raisins, almonds, cinnamon, allspice, sugar and more butter. I held my breath as her hands coaxed an edge of the floured pastry up from the tablecloth. I never believed that anything so thin could hold the filling—the apples were dimly visible through the pastry. She rolled the dough up like a jelly roll. The *roulade*, when she finished, was over three feet long, more than enough to fashion into a giant horseshoe. She sealed the ends of the strudel, applied her goose feather brush once more and baked it.

I remember the whole process as a combination of agonizing wait and quick, greedy pleasure. Three hours to make, eaten in minutes. It was time well-spent, on both our parts.

On a good day, Ritz-Carlton diners consume between twenty and thirty dessert soufflés (each serving two to six people), about five chocolate mousse cakes, a slightly smaller number of pumpkin cheesecakes and several gallons each of strawberries Romanoff and *crème caramel*. To this total I must also add the specially commissioned cakes and ice cream bombes, as well as the several hundred portions from the twenty cakes and pastries, the puddings, coupes and compotes I haven't mentioned. To put it in perspective, if you kidnapped the staff of a popular pastry shop, imprisoned them in our kitchen with instructions not to decrease their daily output by so much as as slice of apple tart, our diners would eat it all—and clamor for more.

Grand Marnier Soufflé

Soufflé au Grand Marnier

Serves 4

Soufflé au Grand Marnier is the signature dessert of The Ritz-Carlton, Boston. Its elegant appeal inevitably sets off a chain reaction in The Dining Room. As soon as we serve one, the waiters begin pouring into the kitchen with orders for a dozen more.

4 tablespoons unsalted butter
2 tablespoons + ½ cup sugar
2 cups milk
3 tablespoons flour
2 tablespoons cornstarch
6 egg yolks, from large eggs
¼ cup + 2 tablespoons Grand Marnier
8 egg whites, from large eggs
1 cup *crème anglaise,* flavored with 2 tablespoons Grand Marnier
  (See recipe on page 148.)

Preheat oven to 375 degrees.

You can use a 2- or 3-quart soufflé dish for this recipe. If you're using the larger soufflé dish, proceed directly to the next paragraph. If you use the smaller size, you'll have to make a collar so the dish can hold all the soufflé mixture. Figuring the dimensions of the collar is easy. Wrap a piece of string around the outside of the dish to measure its circumference. The collar should be 1⅓ times as long as the string, long enough to wrap around the dish and still overlap. Multiply the height of the dish by 4 to get the width of the collar. Now cut the collar out of foil or parchment paper. Fold the collar in half lengthwise. Rub 1 side with ½ tablespoon of butter. Coat the *inside* of the soufflé dish with ½ tablespoon of butter as well. Wrap the collar around the *outside* of the dish, folded edge up, so that the buttered surface of the collar faces the dish. Tie a piece of string around the middle of the collar to hold it in place. If necessary, secure the collar with a paper clip where its ends overlap at the top. Dust the soufflé dish and the collar with 2 tablespoons of the sugar.

If you use a 3-quart dish, coat it with 1 tablespoon of butter and then dust it with 2 tablespoons of the sugar.

Combine the remaining butter and sugar and the milk, flour and cornstarch in a saucepan and bring to a boil, stirring constantly, over high heat. As soon as the mixture boils, reduce the heat to medium-low and cook until the mixture becomes quite thick, stirring constantly (about 5 minutes). Remove the saucepan from the heat, pour the mixture into a large bowl and allow it to cool for 10 minutes. Beat the egg yolks into the mixture one at a time, completely incorporating each yolk before adding the next. Stir in the Grand Marnier.

Whip the egg whites until stiff but not dry. Fold the whites into the egg yolk mixture. Gently pour the batter into the prepared dish. Bake in the center of the oven for 45–50 minutes, until the soufflé puffs above the mold (or collar, for the 2-quart size).

TO SERVE: The soufflé will remain puffed up for only a few minutes, so serve it immediately. Ladle ¼ cup of crème anglaise onto each dessert plate, then top with a generous serving of soufflé.

LIGHT CUSTARD SAUCE

Crème Anglaise

Yields 2½ cups

Crème anglaise is the classic complement to a soufflé, but I like it with bread pudding, a slice of fresh tart or a fruit compote as well.

2 cups milk
6 egg yolks, from large eggs
½ cup sugar
1 teaspoon vanilla
⅛ teaspoon salt

Bring the milk to a boil in a saucepan over high heat. Immediately remove the pan from the heat and cover to keep the milk warm.

Combine the egg yolks, sugar, vanilla and salt in a second saucepan and beat them until well-blended. While continuing to beat the egg yolk mixture, slowly add the scalded milk. Place the pan over low heat and stir constantly with a wooden spoon until the sauce thickens. This can take up to 30 minutes. The end result should be a lovely silky sauce, about the consistency of heavy cream. Remove the pan from the heat and set it into a bath of ice water to stop the cooking, continuing to stir for about 4 minutes. Remove the pan from the ice bath and chill the sauce for 30 minutes before serving.

FLAVORING THE SAUCE: Crème anglaise may be flavored in two different ways: by adding 3–4 tablespoons of your favorite liqueur or spirit to the finished product (e.g., brandy, Grand Marnier, Frangelico); or by adding an ingredient to the milk as you're scalding it. Grated citrus rind (2 tablespoons), instant coffee (1 tablespoon) or melted semisweet chocolate bits (¼–½ cup) produce dramatically different but equally delicious dessert sauces. If you use one of these other flavorings, however, do not omit the vanilla—the other ingredients are in addition to the vanilla, not a substitute for it.

CARAMEL CUSTARD

Crème Caramel

Serves 8

Sometimes, contrary to my best intentions, I don't leave much room for dessert, but I still crave something refreshing. That's when I enjoy *crème caramel*. Every culinary tradition has its own custard recipe. Ours is the classic French version, with caramelized sugar drizzling down the sides.

1¾ cups sugar
½ cup water
6 large eggs
½ teaspoon vanilla
⅛ teaspoon salt
4 cups milk

Preheat oven to 400 degrees.

Combine 1 cup of the sugar with ¼ cup of the water in a heavy-bottomed saucepan. Place the pan over medium heat and cook, without stirring, until all the sugar has melted and caramelized to a golden brown (about 10 minutes). Add the remaining ¼ cup water to the saucepan, taking care not to splatter melted sugar on yourself, and stir until the caramel is completely dissolved and smooth.

Divide the caramelized sugar among 8 custard cups and tilt the cups so the sugar coats the bottoms evenly. Allow the sugar to cool.

Beat together the remaining sugar, the eggs, vanilla and salt in a mixing bowl. Stir in the milk. If the mixture is lumpy, strain it through a sieve. Fill the caramel-lined custard cups with the egg mixture. Place the cups in a roasting pan and add enough hot water to the pan to reach halfway up the custard cups.

Bake the custards in the center of the oven until they set (20–30 minutes).

Remove the custard cups from the water bath, cool them at room temperature, and then place them in the refrigerator to chill at least 1 hour.

TO SERVE: Run a small, thin knife between the custard and the cup. Unmold each crème caramel onto a dessert plate. The caramelized sugar should drizzle from the top of the custard down the sides.

BREAD PUDDING

Pudding au Pain

Serves 4–6

Bread pudding is an old Yankee favorite, alive and well after sixty years of service on our menu.

½ cup raisins
¼ cup Cognac
1 tablespoon unsalted butter
3 cups brioche or French bread cubes, cut into 1″ pieces
6 large eggs
1 teaspoon vanilla
¾ cup sugar
⅛ teaspoon salt
½ teaspoon cinnamon
½ teaspoon freshly grated nutmeg
4 cups milk
¼ cup powdered sugar
1–1¼ cups *crème anglaise* (See recipe on page 148.)

Combine the raisins and the brandy in a small bowl and allow them to macerate for 1 hour.

Preheat oven to 400 degrees.

Coat a 2-quart baking dish with the butter and fill it with the bread cubes.

Beat the eggs, vanilla, sugar, salt, cinnamon and nutmeg together in a large mixing bowl. Stir in the milk and the raisin-brandy mixture. Pour this evenly over the bread cubes.

Bake the pudding until a knife inserted into the center comes out clean (40–50 minutes). Allow it to cool at room temperature, then refrigerate at least 1½ hours to chill thoroughly.

TO SERVE: When you're ready to serve the bread pudding, sprinkle it with powdered sugar. Ladle about ¼ cup of crème anglaise onto each dessert plate, and top with a generous portion of bread pudding. Sprinkle with additional sugar if you like.

CHOCOLATE MOUSSE CAKE

Gâteau de Mousse au Chocolat

Serves 12

Baking mousse produces an extremely dense cake, especially since this recipe contains no flour. Bake the cake a day in advance so that it can chill overnight in the refrigerator, then prepare the frosting on the day you intend to serve it.

MOUSSE CAKE

1½ cups + 1 tablespoon unsalted butter
1 cup semisweet chocolate bits
9 egg yolks, from large eggs
½ cup powdered cocoa
8 egg whites, from large eggs
1½ cups sugar

CHOCOLATE CREAM FROSTING

½ cup semisweet chocolate bits
2 tablespoons water
2 cups heavy cream

GARNISH

½ cup finely ground roasted almonds
¼ cup powdered cocoa
12 chocolate cigarette candies

Preheat oven to 350 degrees.

Coat a 9″ springform pan with 1 tablespoon butter. Line the bottom with a round of parchment paper.

MAKING THE MOUSSE: Melt the semisweet chocolate bits in a saucepan over low heat. Remove the saucepan from the heat.

Put 1½ cups butter in a large mixing bowl. Use an electric mixer to beat the butter until it's fluffy. While continuing to beat the butter, add the egg yolks, 1 yolk at a time, waiting until the previous yolk is well-incorporated before adding the next. Still beating, add the melted chocolate in a slow stream. Last of all, beat in the cocoa. Set aside.

Put the egg whites in a large stainless steel mixing bowl and place the bowl over a saucepan of simmering water. Beat the egg whites until they begin to foam. Beat in the sugar, adding it in a slow steady stream. Once the sugar has dissolved, take the bowl off the saucepan and continue to beat the egg whites until they hold firm (but not dry) peaks.

Fold the egg whites into the chocolate mixture. Put 1 cup of the mousse into a pastry bag and refrigerate. Pour the rest into the prepared springform pan.

Place the springform pan in a roasting pan. Add enough hot water to the roasting pan to reach halfway up the springform pan. Bake in the center of the oven until the cake begins to pull away from the sides of the springform pan (about 50 minutes).

Remove the springform pan from the roasting pan. Do not remove the cake from the springform pan. Allow the cake to cool for 30 minutes.

With the cake still in the springform pan, puncture the top of the cake in 10 or 12 spots and pipe a small amount of the reserved mousse into each hole. Chill the cake in the refrigerator overnight.

MAKING THE FROSTING: Make the frosting the next day. Melt the semisweet chocolate bits with the water in a saucepan over low heat. Remove the pan from the heat. Beat the heavy cream in a large mixing bowl until it holds soft peaks. Stir in the melted chocolate, making sure there aren't any lumps. Place all but 1½ cups of the frosting in a pastry bag with a plain tip.

Remove the springform ring from around the cake. Frost the unmolded cake with the chocolate cream remaining in the mixing bowl. Apply the ground almonds all the way around the side of the cake. Use the chocolate cream in the pastry bag to pipe a spiral, from the center to within 1½″ from the edge of the cake. Dust the spiral with cocoa. Pipe 12 rosettes around the top edge of the cake. Arrange chocolate cigarette candies in a spoke-like fashion atop the rosettes.

Boston Cream Pie

Serves 8–10

CHIFFON CAKE

1¼ cups cake flour, sifted before measuring
1 teaspoon baking powder
¾ cup sugar
½ teaspoon salt
¼ cup vegetable oil
⅓ cup water
4 egg yolks, from large eggs
4 egg whites, from large eggs

PASTRY CREAM

½ cup sugar
2 teaspoons gelatin
¼ cup cornstarch
2 cups light cream
4 large eggs
2 cups heavy cream

FROSTING

2 cups heavy cream
¾ pound semisweet chocolate bits
1 cup unsalted pistachio nuts, peeled and coarsely chopped

Preheat oven to 350 degrees.

MAKING THE CHIFFON CAKE: Line the bottom of an ungreased 9″ springform pan with a round of parchment paper.

Combine the flour, baking powder, ½ cup of the sugar and the salt in a large mixing bowl. Add the oil, water and egg yolks, beating until the batter is smooth and free of lumps. Do not overbeat.

Beat the egg whites in a clean mixing bowl until they begin to foam. Still beating, add the remaining ¼ cup of sugar in a steady stream. Stop beating when the egg whites hold firm (but not dry) peaks.

Stir one-third of the egg whites into the yolk mixture, and then gently fold in the rest of the whites.

Pour the cake batter into the prepared pan. Bake in the center of the oven until the cake begins to pull away from the sides of the pan and springs back when it is lightly pressed (30–35 minutes). Allow the cake to cool completely before removing the ring from the springform pan.

MAKING THE PASTRY CREAM: Combine the sugar, gelatin and cornstarch in a saucepan. Slowly whisk in the light cream and then place the pan over medium-low heat. Stirring constantly, cook the mixture until it begins to thicken (about 15 minutes).

Beat the eggs together in a small bowl. Stir ½ cup of the cream mixture into the eggs to warm them. Then pour the egg mixture into the cream mixture. Still stirring, cook the egg-cream mixture for 4–5 minutes, or until it thickens and becomes smooth. Remove the pan from the heat and cool to room temperature.

At this point, the pastry cream can be refrigerated and kept for a day. When you're ready to finish the cake, warm the pastry cream slowly in a saucepan over low heat to relax the gelatin, then allow it to cool to room temperature.

Whip the heavy cream in a large mixing bowl until it holds soft (but not dry) peaks. Fold it into the pastry cream.

MAKING THE FROSTING: Bring the 2 cups of heavy cream to a boil in a saucepan over high heat. As soon as the cream begins to boil, add the chocolate and reduce the heat to low. Stir until the chocolate has melted and remove the pan from the heat. Continue stirring for 4 minutes to cool the frosting. Allow the frosting to cool to the point where it is still spreadable, but not runny.

ASSEMBLING THE CREAM PIE: Unmold the cake and slice it into 3 layers. Spread the pastry cream between the cake layers and on the sides of the cake. Spread the top of the cake with a thick layer of the chocolate frosting. Decorate the outer edge of the top cake layer with the pistachio nuts. Chill the cake for at least 1 hour before serving.

INDIAN PUDDING

Pudding Indien

Serves 8

Years ago, half the restaurants in New England served Indian pudding, and each had a different recipe. You can still find this pudding quite frequently, but more often than not it's canned. Few kitchens are willing to take the time to make it anymore. Perhaps that explains why so many of our patrons will order a meal of classic French dishes, and then finish their evening with this distinctly American dessert.

4 cups milk
¼ teaspoon salt
½ cup + 2 tablespoons yellow cornmeal
4 large eggs
¼ cup sugar
¼ cup brown sugar
¾ cup molasses
½ teaspoon ground ginger
¼ teaspoon cinnamon
⅛ teaspoon freshly grated nutmeg
¾ cup heavy cream
2 tablespoons unsalted butter, melted
¼ cup powdered sugar
1 pint vanilla ice cream

Bring the milk to a boil in a large saucepan over high heat. Turn the heat to low. When the milk is simmering, add the salt and the cornmeal in a slow steady stream, stirring constantly. If you add the cornmeal too quickly it will lump. Cook slowly, stirring frequently, for 45 minutes.

Preheat oven to 350 degrees.

Beat the eggs in a mixing bowl and add the remaining ingredients, except the powdered sugar and the ice cream. When the egg mixture is well blended, slowly add the cornmeal mixture, one spoonful at a time.

Pour the pudding into 8 custard cups or earthenware pudding dishes. Put the dishes in a roasting pan and add enough hot water to the pan to reach halfway up the dishes. Cover the pan with a piece of parchment or brown paper and bake in the center of the oven until the pudding is set (45–50 minutes).

TO SERVE: Serve hot, sprinkled with powdered sugar and topped with a small scoop of vanilla ice cream.

PUMPKIN CHEESECAKE

Serves 12

Plan on making this cheesecake a day or so in advance so it can rest for at least twenty-four hours in the refrigerator before you serve it.

1 tablespoon unsalted butter
½ cup fine gingersnap crumbs
2 pounds cream cheese, softened
1½ cups brown sugar
5 large eggs
¼ cup flour
1 teaspoon cinnamon
1 teaspoon allspice
1 teaspoon ground ginger
¼ teaspoon salt
2 cups canned pumpkin purée
¼ cup pure maple syrup
½ cup walnut halves

Preheat oven to 325 degrees.

Coat a 9″ springform pan with the butter. Sprinkle the gingersnap crumbs in the pan and tilt the pan to cover the bottom and the sides evenly with the crumbs.

In a large mixing bowl, beat the cream cheese until fluffy. Gradually beat in the sugar. Add the eggs, 1 at a time, beating well after each addition. Sift the dry ingredients into the bowl and mix them into the cheese mixture. Add the pumpkin purée and blend well.

Pour the batter into the prepared pan and bake in the center of the oven for 1¾–2 hours. The cake is done when the sides pull away from the pan and a toothpick inserted into the center of the cake comes out clean.

Allow the cake to cool on a rack at room temperature for 1 hour, then remove the ring from the springform pan. Keep the cake at room temperature until it has cooled completely. Then cover it with plastic wrap and chill it in the refrigerator overnight.

TO SERVE: Just before serving, brush the top with the maple syrup and encircle the outer edge with the walnut halves.

Peach Melba

Pêches Melba

Serves 4

1 chiffon cake made in a 10″ x 14″ pan (See recipe on page 152.)
2 large ripe peaches
½ lemon

MELBA SAUCE

1 pint raspberries
1 tablespoon lemon juice
¼ cup sugar
½ cup heavy cream

1 pint vanilla ice cream

16 fresh raspberries, for garnish
2 tablespoons unsalted pistachio nuts, peeled and coarsely chopped,
   for garnish

Preheat oven to 350 degrees.

MAKING THE CHIFFON CAKE: Line the bottom of a 10″ x 14″ ungreased pan with parchment paper. Prepare the chiffon cake batter according to the instructions on page 153. Check the cake after 20 minutes of baking because it will cook faster in this pan.

After the cake has cooled, remove it from the pan and cut 4 circles out of it, 4″ in diameter. Save the excess cake for another use.

PREPARING THE PEACHES: Bring 2 quarts of water to a boil in a saucepan over high heat. Add the peaches and boil for 30 seconds. Immediately plunge the peaches into ice water to stop the cooking. When the peaches have cooled, slip off the skins, cut the peaches in half and remove the pits. Place the halves in a bowl, cover with water, and squeeze the juice of ½ a lemon into the water to keep them from discoloring until they are to be served.

MAKING THE MELBA SAUCE: Combine the pint of raspberries, the tablespoon of lemon juice and the sugar in a food processor or a blender. Blend until well puréed. If you prefer a seedless sauce, strain the purée through a fine sieve.

Whip the heavy cream until it holds firm peaks, and place it in a pastry bag with a star tip.

TO SERVE: Place the cake rounds in 4 dessert bowls. Top each portion of cake with a scoop of ice cream. Set a peach half on top of the ice cream and spoon ¼ cup of Melba sauce over the peach. Pipe a decorative rosette of whipped cream onto the peach. Garnish each dish with 4 fresh raspberries and some pistachio nuts.

COFFEE POT DE CRÈME

Pot de Crème au Café

Serves 8

1 tablespoon instant coffee
1 tablespoon hot water
1½ cups milk
1½ cups light cream
¾ cup sugar
4 large eggs
4 egg yolks, from large eggs
⅛ teaspoon salt
1 cup heavy cream

Preheat oven to 325 degrees.

Mix the instant coffee with the hot water.

Bring the milk and cream to a boil in a saucepan over high heat. Remove the pan from the heat and allow the mixture to cool slightly.

Mix the coffee, sugar, eggs, egg yolks and salt together in a large mixing bowl and beat well with a wire whisk. Still beating, add the scalded milk-cream mixture in a steady stream. When everything is well-blended, strain the mixture through a sieve into another bowl. Let stand for 15 minutes and skim off any foam that rises to the surface.

Fill 8 custard cups with the coffee custard and place them in a roasting pan. Add enough hot water to the roasting pan to reach halfway up the custard cups. Cover the pan with a sheet of foil and bake until the custard is set (about 30 minutes). Remove the cups from the hot water bath. Allow them to cool to room temperature and then chill them in the refrigerator for at least 1 hour.

TO SERVE: Whip the heavy cream until it holds firm peaks. Place it in a pastry bag with a star tip and pipe a decorative rosette on each *pot de crème*.

Apple Strudel

Strudel aux Pommes

•

Serves 8–10

DOUGH

1¾ cups flour
1 large egg
⅓ cup warm water
1 tablespoon unsalted butter, melted
¼ teaspoon salt

FILLING

6 cups apples, peeled, cored and sliced ⅛″ thick (about 2 pounds)
½ cup sugar
1 teaspoon cinnamon
½ cup coarsely chopped walnuts
½ cup white raisins
1 tablespoon lemon juice
2 teaspoons grated lemon rind
¾ cup unsalted butter, melted
1 cup dry bread crumbs

3 tablespoons unsalted butter, melted
Flour for rolling out the dough
1 cup heavy cream
¼ cup powdered sugar

MAKING THE DOUGH: Combine all of the dough ingredients in the bowl of a food processor with a plastic blade. Blend for 3 minutes, adding more flour if the dough is too sticky. Wrap the dough in a damp cloth and allow it to rest in a warm place for 30 minutes.

MAKING THE FILLING: Combine all of the filling ingredients, except ½ cup of the melted butter and the bread crumbs, in a bowl. Mix well and allow to macerate for 30 minutes, stirring frequently.

Combine the ½ cup of melted butter with the bread crumbs in a sauté pan and cook over medium heat until the crumbs are toasted and golden brown (about 5 minutes). Remove the pan from the heat and allow the crumbs to cool.

Preheat oven to 350 degrees. Grease a baking sheet with 1 tablespoon of melted butter.

You will need a very large work area, such as a kitchen table, and a large cloth, about 4′ square, for this project.

Spread the cloth on the work surface and dust it liberally with flour. Place the dough in the center of the cloth and roll it into a 30″ square. You will have to stop and dust both sides of the dough with flour several times to keep it from sticking to the cloth.

STRETCHING THE DOUGH: Put the rolling pin aside. Part of the appeal of a good strudel is its amazingly flaky crust, the result of many extremely thin layers of dough. You're now going to stretch the dough by hand until it's so thin you can virtually read through it. Although you'll be working with a very thin sheet of pastry, it's elastic and won't break easily. If you do poke a hole in it, you can easily patch it with a scrap of dough, using your finger, dipped in water, to seal the edges. If you're doing this for the first time, remember that with practice it will become easier for you. Don't become discouraged. There's nothing quite like a flaky homemade strudel.

To stretch the dough, first dust your hands with flour, then place the backs of your hands in the center of the underside of the dough. Slowly and gently move your hands out from the center of the dough to the edges, stretching the dough in the process. Rotate the dough one-eighth of a turn and repeat the stretching procedure. Continue to stretch the dough until it's very thin and translucent. The finished sheet should measure about 3′ square.

Using a sharp knife, cut the dough into a 30″ square. Use the trimmings to patch any holes. Leave the dough on the cloth for the next step.

ASSEMBLING THE STRUDEL: Spread the bread crumbs evenly over the dough. Leave a 4″ swath of dough uncovered at the top and bottom. Mound the apple mixture in a single row, 3–4 inches wide, atop the lower edge of the crumb mixture. (Don't let the apples spill onto the space of uncovered dough.) Leave a couple of inches of uncovered crumb mixture at both ends of the row of filling.

To roll the strudel, grasp the edge of the cloth and flip it, with the dough, over the filling. Continue to pull the edge of the cloth up and away from you, rolling the strudel at the same time. The first roll should completely encase the apple filling in the dough. Continue to roll the strudel, pulling the cloth away from you, until all the dough is used up. Fold the ends of the roll under.

Transfer the strudel, seam side down, to a buttered baking sheet and bend it into a horseshoe shape. Brush the top with 2 tablespoons of melted butter. Bake in the center of the oven until golden brown (about 50–60 minutes). Remove from the oven and let cool until just warm.

TO SERVE: Cut the strudel into 1½″ slices. Place 1 slice on each dessert plate. Pour a tablespoon of heavy cream over one corner of each portion and dust with powdered sugar.

PEARS POACHED IN PORT

Poires Pochées au Porto

Serves 6

6 ripe pears
2 cups port
4 cups water
2 cinnamon sticks
½ cup lemon juice
1 cup sugar
¾ cup heavy cream

6 sprigs fresh mint, for garnish
12 candied violets, for garnish

Peel the pears and remove the cores with an apple corer. Put the pears in a bowl and cover with cold water, so they don't discolor.

Bring the port, water, cinnamon sticks, lemon juice and sugar to a boil in a large saucepan over high heat. Reduce the heat to medium-low, add the pears and simmer until they are easily pierced with a knife (15–20 minutes). They should remain firm.

Remove the pears from the cooking liquid and let cool to room temperature. Cover the pears with plastic wrap and chill in the refrigerator.

Cook the poaching liquid over medium heat until it is syrupy and reduced to about 1½ cups (about 40 minutes). Remove the cinnamon sticks and chill the syrup.

TO SERVE: Whip the heavy cream until it holds firm peaks. Place it in a pastry bag with a star tip. Pour a small pool of the syrup onto each of 6 chilled dessert plates. Place a pear, upright, on each plate. Pipe a rosette of whipped cream atop each pear and garnish with 2 candied violets. Place a sprig of mint at the bottom of the plate.

BLUEBERRY MUFFINS

Yields 12

We usually serve muffins for breakfast, but I happen to think that our blueberry muffins—when accompanied by a scoop of vanilla ice cream—make a great summer dessert. Follow the recipe and you'll have not only muffins for dessert, but enough for breakfast as well.

8 tablespoons unsalted butter
5 large eggs
½ cup milk
3½ cups flour, sifted before measuring
2 tablespoons + 1 teaspoon baking powder
1½ cups sugar
⅛ teaspoon salt
4 cups fresh blueberries (or 24 ounces unsweetened, frozen,
  defrosted)
1 pint vanilla ice cream

Use 2 tablespoons of butter to coat 12 muffin molds and line the molds with paper baking cups.

Melt the remaining 6 tablespoons of butter in a small saucepan over medium heat.

Beat the eggs in a mixing bowl until well-blended. Add the melted butter and the milk.

In a large mixing bowl, combine the flour, baking powder, ¾ cup sugar and the salt. Add the egg mixture to the dry ingredients and mix until they are well-blended, but do not over-mix or the muffins will be tough. Fold in the blueberries.

Cover the bowl with plastic wrap and refrigerate for 2 hours.

Preheat oven to 400 degrees.

Spoon the blueberry muffin batter into the baking cups so that it mounds about ¼″ above the level of each cup. The batter will be stiff enough so that it doesn't spread out. Sprinkle each muffin generously with about a tablespoon of sugar. Bake in the center of the oven for 25–30 minutes, or until the tops are golden brown.

TO SERVE: Serve the muffins warm. Split them in half. Top each half with a small scoop of ice cream.

VANILLA-RASPBERRY ICE CREAM MOLD

Bombe Glacée Cyrano aux Framboises

Serves 8

Ice cream molds (or bombes) enjoyed a great fashion in the nineteenth century and then their culinary appeal faded. Recent emphasis on dramatic, contrasting colors and textures has made them popular again. We serve oversized bombes for large private parties. This particular recipe, scaled down to dinner-party size, marries the tart flavor of raspberries with the richness of vanilla ice cream.

1 quart vanilla ice cream
1 pint raspberry sorbet
1 cup heavy cream

RASPBERRY SAUCE

1 pint fresh raspberries (or 12 ounces unsweetened frozen,
  defrosted)
½ cup sugar
¼–½ cup framboise liqueur

1 cup fresh raspberries, for garnish
24 candied violets, for garnish

ASSEMBLING THE BOMBE: Pack a 2-quart freezer-proof bowl with a layer of vanilla ice cream. The ice cream layer should be about 1½″ thick and conform to the shape of the bowl, leaving room for the sorbet. Freeze the bowl until the ice cream is firm.

Fill the lined bowl with the raspberry sorbet and freeze until firm.

Whip the heavy cream until it holds firm peaks. Place it in a pastry bag with a star tip. Refrigerate the bag until you're ready to use it.

MAKING THE RASPBERRY SAUCE: Combine the sauce ingredients in a saucepan (use ¼ or ½ cup framboise according to your own taste) and bring to a boil over high heat. Reduce the heat to low and simmer for 6–8 minutes. Strain the sauce through a sieve to remove the seeds.

TO SERVE: When you're ready to serve the bombe, dip the bowl in warm water. As soon as the ice cream is released from the sides of the bowl, unmold the bombe onto a serving plate. Decorate the bombe with small rosettes of whipped cream. Garnish with the raspberries and the candied violets. Cut the bombe into wedges, place them on dessert plates and spoon some raspberry sauce over half of each wedge.

CHESTNUT SUNDAE

Coupe aux Marrons

Serves 4

½ cup heavy cream
16 candied chestnuts
1 pint vanilla ice cream
4 tablespoons dark rum

Whip the heavy cream until it holds firm peaks and place it in a pastry bag with a star tip. Refrigerate the bag until you're ready to use it.

Set 4 of the candied chestnuts aside for garnish. Chop the rest of them coarsely. Divide the chopped chestnuts into 4 equal portions, then arrange them in the bottoms of 4 parfait glasses. Add a scoop of ice cream to each glass, then sprinkle each with a tablespoon of rum. Pipe a decorative rosette of whipped cream on the ice cream and top with a candied chestnut.

STRAWBERRIES WITH MANGO PURÉE

Fraises, Purée de Mangue

Serves 6

3 pints strawberries
6 ripe mangos
Sugar and lemon juice to taste
½ cup pistachio nuts, peeled and coarsely chopped

Wash and hull the strawberries. Drain of excess water.

Peel the mangos and cut the meat off the pit. Purée the mangos in a food processor or blender until smooth. Taste the purée and season it with sugar and lemon juice, if necessary.

TO SERVE: Pour a small pool of mango purée on each of 6 chilled dessert plates. Place the strawberries, stem end down, on the purée, and sprinkle with the pistachio nuts.

STRAWBERRIES ROMANOFF

Fraises Romanoff

Serves 6

2 quarts strawberries
¼ cup Grand Marnier
2 cups port
¼ cup + 3 tablespoons sugar
3 cups heavy cream

Wash and hull the strawberries and cut them in half. Mix the Grand Marnier, port and ¼ cup of the sugar in a large bowl and add the strawberries. Let the strawberries macerate for at least 2 hours in the refrigerator.

Whip the cream with the remaining 3 tablespoons of sugar in a large bowl until it holds soft peaks. Place 1 cup of the cream in a pastry bag with a star tip. Refrigerate the bag until you're ready to use it.

Drain the strawberries and discard the liquid. Fold the berries into the whipped cream.

TO SERVE: Divide the strawberries and cream among 6 chilled dessert bowls. Top each portion with a decorative rosette of whipped cream.

CHAPTER 12

RECIPES FROM OTHER RITZ-CARLTONS

A quick visit to the kitchens of the other Ritz-Carlton Hotels immediately demonstrates that no culinary precept—except a commitment to quality—is graven in stone. The chefs at the other hotels have in common a background that includes formal training in European cooking schools, but each has responded to the challenges of his particular hotel in his own resourceful manner.

Chef Bruno Mella received his formal training at the Westminster Catering College in London. As head of a kitchen at a resort hotel—The Ritz-Carlton in Naples, Florida—he discovered that vacationing guests can be more demanding than business travelers. While he appreciates the restraint of *nouvelle cuisine*, he has also observed that people on vacation will treat themselves to a rich dish that they might avoid the rest of the year.

Atlanta is unique in that it boasts *two* Ritz-Carlton Hotels, Atlanta and Buckhead. Before coming to the former, Chef Josef Lageder was already a star. The Restaurant Writers Association of California voted Ravelle, the Los Angeles restaurant where he then presided, as the best new restaurant of 1983. Quite an honor in California, a state that fosters culinary celebrities. Chef Lageder began his career with formal training in Austria, then worked in Houston, Hawaii and Los Angeles before coming to Atlanta. His talent for locating purveyors with the finest regional products has always enabled him to create sophisticated menus with a distinctively Southern flavor, while still incorporating the Asian influence of California and Hawaii.

François LeCoin, chef at Buckhead, remains dedicated to the classic cuisine of his native France. Chef LeCoin's family owned a small restaurant in Chartres, and he has little patience with cooking that emphasises innovation simply for the sake of producing something new, often at the expense of the ingredients. The beauty of classic technique, in Chef LeCoin's opinion, is its adaptability to regional circumstances, guaranteeing delicious results no matter what the ingredients, as long as they're fresh and of high quality.

As an ardent jogger, skier and tennis player, Chef Christian Russinoux epitomizes the healthy Californian. Guests at The Ritz-Carlton, Laguna Niguel appreciate the West Coast influence in his cooking—an openness to other culinary approaches and an emphasis on highlighting the natural flavors of the ingredients. Not that he has abandoned his roots. Chef Russinoux's confit of duck might seem native to Paris (where he received his formal training), but his pasta appetizer contains elements native to both France and the American Southwest, and the breast of chicken with shiitakes and baby bok choy could only have emerged from the culture of Southern California.

The Ritz-Carlton, Naples

Naples, Florida

Pheasant Consommé

Oyster and Scallop Casserole with Saffron Sauce

Florida Lobster Strudel

Avocado and Grapefruit Salad

Original Key Lime Pie

Pheasant Consommé

Serves 4

½ pound lean pheasant meat, cut into ⅛″ pieces
1 egg white, from a large egg
3 tablespoons onions, diced into ¼″ pieces
2 tablespoons carrots, diced into ¼″ pieces
3 tablespoons celery, diced into ¼″ pieces
2 parsley stems (not the leaves), finely chopped
1 small bay leaf, crumbled
½ teaspoon finely chopped fresh thyme (or ¼ teaspoon dried)
¼ teaspoon black peppercorns
4 cups cold, fat-free veal stock (See recipe on page 30.)
Salt to taste
2–4 tablespoons Madeira, optional

1 black truffle, for garnish

In a cool, heavy-bottomed stock pot beat the pheasant meat and egg white together with a heavy spoon until they're a frothy mass. Add the remaining ingredients, except the salt, Madeira and truffle, and bring the pot to a boil over high heat, constantly stirring and scraping the bottom to make sure nothing sticks.

As soon as the pot begins to boil, stop stirring! Reduce the heat to low and let the pot simmer *slowly* for 1 hour. As the stock bubbles, the egg white hardens around the solid bits of vegetables, meat and other particles that would cloud the stock. The bubbling action carries the particles to the surface, where they form a solid "raft."

After the consommé has simmered for 1½ hours, carefully lift off the raft of coagulated egg white. Strain the broth through 4 layers of rinsed cheesecloth and season with salt. Add 2–4 tablespoons of Madeira, if you prefer a darker, richer consommé.

TO SERVE: Ladle 1 cup of consommé into each of 4 heated soup bowls. Using a potato peeler, shave 2 or 3 paper-thin slices of truffle into each serving.

Oyster and Scallop Casserole with Saffron Sauce

Serves 4

SAFFRON SAUCE

1 tablespoon + ½ pound unsalted butter, cut into ½" cubes
1 tablespoon minced shallots
½ cup dry white wine
¼ teaspoon saffron threads, crumbled
1 cup fish stock (See recipe on page 32.)
½ cup heavy cream
Salt and freshly ground white pepper to taste

OYSTER AND SCALLOP CASSEROLE

1 pound spinach
2 tablespoons unsalted butter
Salt and freshly ground white pepper to taste
¼ cup carrots, cut into julienne strips 2" x ⅛"
¼ cup celery, cut into julienne strips 2" x ⅛"
¼ cup leeks, cut into julienne strips 2" x ⅛"
12 sea scallops
12 oysters, shucked
⅓ cup Pernod

MAKING THE SAUCE: Melt 1 tablespoon of butter in a saucepan over medium heat. Add the shallots and cook until translucent (about 3 minutes). Remove the pan from the heat and add the wine and saffron. Return the pan to medium heat. Reduce the mixture until only 1 tablespoon of liquid remains (about 10 minutes). Take care not to let the liquid boil away.

Add the fish stock and reduce it by half, then add the heavy cream and reduce it by half as well. Turn the heat to low. Whisk in the remaining ½ pound butter, 1 cube at a time, emulsifying the butter with the reduction. *Do not boil! If the sauce boils, the emulsion will separate!* Season with salt and pepper. Strain the sauce through a fine sieve into a clean saucepan and cover to keep warm while you prepare the casserole.

MAKING THE CASSEROLE: To prepare the spinach, grasp each leaf by the stem. Pinch the undersides of the leaf together and pull the stem upward through the leaf. In addition to eliminating the stem, this technique removes the fibrous vein that runs through the leaf. Rinse the leaves thoroughly under cold running water to remove any sand or grit. Air-dry the spinach or pat it dry with paper towels.

Preheat oven to 450 degrees.

Melt 1 tablespoon of the butter in a large sauté pan over high heat. Add the spinach, season with salt and pepper and toss until the spinach has just wilted (about 3 minutes).

Drain the spinach in a colander, then distribute it equally among 4 small oven-proof casserole dishes.

Bring a small pot of salted water to a boil over high heat. Add the julienned vegetables and cook for 2 minutes. Tip the vegetables into a colander and immediately rinse under cold running water to stop the cooking. Pat the vegetables dry and set aside.

Melt 1 tablespoon of butter in a large sauté pan over medium-high heat. Add the scallops and sauté until barely cooked (4–5 minutes). Don't let them brown. Transfer 3 scallops to each casserole dish. In the same sauté pan, over medium-high heat, cook the oysters for 3 minutes. Transfer 3 oysters to each dish, leaving any liquid in the pan. Remove the sauté pan from the heat. Add the Pernod to the pan and return to medium-high heat. Cook until the Pernod has reduced by half, then take the pan off the heat. Add the saffron sauce to the pan, combine it with the Pernod and ladle about ¼ cup of the sauce into each of the casserole dishes. Sprinkle each dish with some of the julienned vegetables, and place the dishes in the oven for 2–3 minutes (no longer or the sauce will separate). Serve immediately.

Florida Lobster Strudel

Serves 4

STRUDELS

3 tablespoons unsalted butter
1 tablespoon minced shallots
1 pound white mushrooms, diced into ¼" pieces
Salt and freshly ground white pepper to taste
1 pound spinach
1 pound puff pastry (available in 1-pound packages at grocery
    stores)
4 cooked Florida lobster tails, approximately 10 ounces each,
    cooked and shelled
1 large egg
1 tablespoon water

CREAM SAUCE

1 tablespoon unsalted butter + ¾ pound unsalted butter, cut into
    ½" cubes, chilled
1 tablespoon minced shallots
½ cup dry white wine
¼ cup white wine vinegar
1 bay leaf, whole
1½ cups heavy cream
Salt and freshly ground white pepper to taste
Lemon juice to taste

GARNISH

2 teaspoons red salmon roe
2 teaspoons American sturgeon black caviar
4 sprigs parsley

MAKING THE STRUDELS: Preheat oven to 425 degrees.

Melt 2 tablespoons of the butter in a large sauté pan over medium-high heat. Add the shallots and mushrooms and cook, stirring frequently, until no more liquid is exuded from the vegetables (8–10 minutes). Remove the pan from the heat, season the mushroom mixture with salt and pepper and allow it to cool.

To prepare the spinach, grasp each leaf by the stem. Pinch the undersides of the leaf together and pull the stem upward through the leaf. In addition to eliminating the stem, this technique removes the fibrous vein that runs through the leaf. Rinse the leaves thoroughly in cold running water to remove any sand or grit. Air-dry the spinach or pat it dry with paper towels.

Melt the remaining tablespoon of the butter in a large sauté pan over high heat. Add the spinach, season with salt and pepper, and toss until the spinach has just wilted (about 3 minutes). Drain the spinach in a colander and allow it to cool.

If you purchased a commercial 1-pound package of puff pastry, you should have 2 sheets. Roll out each sheet to a thickness of ⅛″. You should have enough pastry to cut 4 rectangles, each measuring 10″ x 12″.

Cover half of each rectangle (across the narrow width) with one-eighth of the spinach. Leave a ½″ margin of pastry uncovered around the edges of the rectangle. Spread one-eighth of the mushroom mixture over the spinach and then top with a lobster tail. Cover each tail with one-eighth of the mushrooms and then finish with the remaining spinach.

Beat the egg with the water and use it to brush the ½″ border of exposed pastry. Fold the uncovered half of the rectangle over the vegetables and lobster tail. Pinch the seams to seal them tight. Place the strudels on an ungreased baking sheet. Brush them with the egg wash and poke 3 small holes in the top of each one. Bake until golden brown (about 15 minutes). Allow them to rest 10 minutes before serving.

MAKING THE SAUCE: Melt the tablespoon of butter in a saucepan over medium heat. Add the shallots and cook for 3 minutes. Remove the pan from the heat, then add the white wine, vinegar and bay leaf. Return the pan to medium heat. Cook until 1 tablespoon of liquid remains (about 10 minutes). Add the cream and reduce it by half (about 10 minutes). Turn the heat to low and whisk in the butter, 1 cube at a time, emulsifying the butter with the reduction. *Do not boil! If the sauce boils, the emulsion will separate!* Season with salt, pepper and lemon juice. Strain the sauce through a fine sieve into a warmed sauce boat.

TO SERVE: Cut each strudel crosswise into 4 equal slices. Ladle ¼ cup of sauce onto each of 4 warmed dinner plates. Place ½ teaspoon of salmon roe in the center of each plate and arrange the strudel medallions around it. Set ⅛ teaspoon of sturgeon caviar on top of each medallion and garnish the plates with a sprig of parsley.

AVOCADO AND GRAPEFRUIT SALAD

Serves 4

HAZELNUT VINAIGRETTE

½ tablespoon black peppercorns
2 tablespoons minced shallots
1 tablespoon finely chopped fresh thyme (or ½ tablespoon dried)
2 tablespoons finely chopped fresh basil (or 1 tablespoon dried)
¼ cup balsamic vinegar
1 tablespoon sherry vinegar
½ tablespoon Dijon mustard
½ cup + 2 tablespoons hazelnut oil
¼ cup olive oil
1 tablespoon chicken stock (See recipe on page 31.)
Salt to taste

SALAD

2 avocados
2 grapefruits

8 chives, cut into 6″ lengths, for garnish
½ cup hazelnuts, toasted and peeled, for garnish

MAKING THE VINAIGRETTE: Rock a heavy-bottomed saucepan over the peppercorns to crack them, then put them into the saucepan. Add the shallots, thyme, basil and vinegars to the pan, and place over medium heat. When the liquid has reduced to 2 tablespoons, remove the pan from the heat.

Using a wire whisk, beat the mustard into the reduction. Then beat in the hazelnut oil, olive oil and chicken stock. Season with salt and cover the pan to keep the sauce warm.

MAKING THE SALAD: Peel the avocados and cut each one into 8 slices. Remove the rind and pith from the grapefruits. Separate the sections, cutting carefully between the membranes. Fan 4 avocado slices on the left side of each of 4 salad plates and 6 grapefruit sections on the right. Cross 2 chives at the bottom of each plate. Sprinkle each salad with 2 tablespoons of hazelnuts and 2–3 tablespoons of warm vinaigrette.

ORIGINAL KEY LIME PIE

PIE SHELL

1½ cups finely ground graham cracker crumbs
6 tablespoons unsalted butter, melted

KEY LIME FILLING

2 egg yolks, from large eggs
15 ounces sweetened condensed milk
½ cup lime juice
½ cup heavy cream

MAKING THE PIE SHELL: Preheat oven to 300 degrees.

Combine the crumbs and the melted butter in a mixing bowl. Press the mixture evenly into a 9″ pie plate. Bake for 15 minutes and then allow to cool before adding the filling.

MAKING THE FILLING AND BAKING THE PIE: Preheat oven to 350 degrees.

Beat the egg yolks in a mixing bowl until they're a light lemon color. Stir in the milk and lime juice and combine the ingredients well.

When the pie shell has cooled, pour the lime filling into the shell and bake the pie until it sets (about 10 minutes). Allow the pie to cool to room temperature, then chill it in the refrigerator for at least 1 hour.

TO SERVE: When you're ready to serve the pie, whip the cream until it holds firm peaks. Place it in a pastry bag with a star tip. Pipe rosettes around the edge of the pie.

THE RITZ-CARLTON, BUCKHEAD

ATLANTA, GEORGIA

Vidalia Onion Tart

Georgia Field Salad with Yellow Pear Tomatoes,
Fresh Herb-Lime Vinaigrette

Roast Georgia Quail St. Alexis

Georgia Peach Mousse with Strawberry Coulis

VIDALIA ONION TART

Serves 6

½ pound puff pastry (available in 1-pound packages at grocery
   stores)
3 tablespoons unsalted butter
1 pound Vidalia onions, sliced ¼″ thick
3 large eggs
1½ cups milk
⅛ teaspoon freshly grated nutmeg
Salt and freshly ground white pepper to taste
½ pound Gruyère cheese, diced into ½″ pieces (about 1 cup)

Roll out the puff pastry until it's ⅛″ thick and large enough to fit into a 10″ pie pan. Coat the pie pan with 1 tablespoon of the butter, then fit the pastry into it. Trim the excess pastry and chill the crust for at least 30 minutes.

Melt the remaining 2 tablespoons of butter in a large sauté pan over medium-low heat. Add the onions and cook, stirring frequently, until they're soft, but not brown (about 30 minutes). Drain the onions on paper towels to eliminate any excess moisture that would ruin the tart.

Preheat oven to 325 degrees.

Beat the eggs, milk and nutmeg together. Season this custard mixture with salt and pepper.

Arrange the onions on the pie shell, top them with the cheese and then pour the custard over the pie. Bake until the custard has set (about 45 minutes). Allow the tart to rest 10 minutes before serving.

Georgia Field Salad with Yellow Pear Tomatoes, Fresh Herb-Lime Vinaigrette

Serves 6

¼ pound baby spinach
2 heads baby Bibb lettuce
1 head red oak leaf lettuce
1 head green oak leaf lettuce
¼ pound lamb's lettuce

HERB-LIME VINAIGRETTE

2 teaspoons finely chopped fresh tarragon (or 1 teaspoon dried)
2 teaspoons finely chopped fresh coriander (cilantro)
2 teaspoons finely chopped parsley
¼ cup lime juice
½ cup vegetable oil
Salt and freshly ground white pepper to taste

18 tiny yellow pear tomatoes, cut in half, for garnish
6 sprigs fresh coriander, for garnish

Strip the spinach leaves of stems and wash well. Separate the lettuce leaves from the cores and wash them well. Drain the spinach and lettuce leaves, pat dry and wrap in tea towels. Refrigerate the bundles for 30 minutes to crisp the leaves.

MAKING THE VINAIGRETTE: Combine the herbs and lime juice in a bowl. While beating the mixture with a whisk, add the oil in a steady stream. Season with salt and pepper.

TO SERVE: Arrange the spinach and lettuce leaves on 6 chilled salad plates. Garnish each arrangement with 6 yellow tomato halves and a sprig of coriander. Drizzle about 2 tablespoons of the vinaigrette over each salad.

ROAST GEORGIA QUAIL
ST. ALEXIS

Serves 6

Ask your butcher to bone twelve quail. You want the breast and thigh bones removed and the quail left whole. The leg bones may remain. Because most quail is sold frozen, be sure to call your butcher several days in advance. He (or she) will need time to order the quail and let them thaw before boning them.

QUAIL AND STUFFING

1½ tablespoons unsalted butter
6 ounces chicken livers, cleaned of strings and blood vessels
1 tablespoon minced shallots
2 tablespoons mushrooms, diced into ¼″ pieces
½ teaspoon finely chopped fresh thyme (or ¼ teaspoon dried)
2 tablespoons Cognac
2 tablespoons Madeira
Salt and freshly ground black pepper to taste
6 ounces chicken breast meat, cut into ¼″ pieces
4 ounces high-quality *foie gras*, cut into ¼″ pieces
1 large egg
¼ cup heavy cream
12 quail, whole, boned

WILD RICE

2 tablespoons raisins
¼ cup water
4 cups chicken stock (See recipe on page 31.)
3 tablespoons unsalted butter
2 tablespoons onions, diced into ¼″ pieces
1½ cups wild rice
Salt and freshly ground black pepper to taste

APPLES

4 cups water
1½ cups sugar
3 Golden Delicious apples

SAUCE

7 tablespoons unsalted butter, softened
Salt and freshly ground black pepper to taste
¼ cup + 2 tablespoons Curaçao
2 cups heavy cream
½ pound seedless green grapes
2 tablespoons Cognac

2 tablespoons red currant jelly, for garnish

MAKING THE STUFFING: Melt the butter over high heat in a sauté pan. Add the chicken livers and cook, stirring frequently, for 3 minutes. Transfer the livers to a plate and allow to cool. Add the shallots, mushrooms and thyme to the pan and sauté for 3 minutes. Remove the pan from the heat, add the Cognac and Madeira. Return the pan to the heat and *carefully* flame the alcohol. When the flame subsides, take the pan off the heat, season the mixture with salt and pepper and allow it to cool.

Place the chicken livers, mushroom mixture, chicken pieces, foie gras and egg in the bowl of a food processor. Purée to a smooth paste. Blend in the cream and season with salt and pepper. Do not overprocess the mixture.

STUFFING THE QUAIL: Set a quail, skin-side down, in front of you. Place 1 tablespoon of stuffing in the center. Enclose the stuffing by drawing up the sides of the quail skin and overlapping them by ¼″. Using heavy-duty thread, stitch the overlapping edges together from the head to the tail (down the back of the quail, so that it looks as it did before it was boned). Tie a piece of twine around the wings to pin them against the body. Tie the legs together. Repeat with the remaining quail. Refrigerate the birds until you're ready to cook them, but no longer than 3 hours. (As a precautionary measure against food poisoning, *no* poultry should be stuffed more than 3 hours in advance.)

POACHING THE APPLES: Bring the 4 cups of water and the 1½ cups of sugar to a boil in a saucepan over medium-high heat. Cook for 5 minutes.

Peel the apples, cut them in half and remove the cores. Add them to the sugar water, turn the heat to medium-low and simmer for 10–15 minutes or until they're easily pierced with a knife. They should remain firm. Remove the apples from the cooking liquid and let them cool to room temperature. Set aside.

MAKING THE RICE: Combine the raisins with the ¼ cup of water and allow to soak while the rice is cooking. Bring the chicken stock to a boil over high heat in a saucepan. Remove the pan from the heat and cover it to keep the stock warm.

Melt 2 tablespoons of the butter in a heavy-bottomed saucepan over medium heat. Add the 2 tablespoons of onion and sauté until translucent (about 3 minutes). Add the rice, stirring until the grains are completely coated with butter. Add the heated chicken stock and bring to a boil. Cover the pan, reduce the heat to its lowest point and let the rice and stock cook for 40 minutes, without lifting the lid.

Remove the pan from the heat and let it stand, covered, for 15 minutes, then uncover and drain off any remaining liquid. Drain the raisins and add them and the remaining tablespoon of butter to the rice. Season with salt and pepper.

COOKING THE QUAIL AND MAKING THE SAUCE: Preheat oven to 400 degrees.

Season the quail with salt and pepper. Melt 2 tablespoons of the butter in each of 2 large oven-proof sauté pans over high heat. Place the quails, breast-side down, in the pans. Sauté until the breasts have browned (4–5 minutes), then put the pans into the oven. Roast the quail for 7–10 minutes. The quail has finished cooking when a skewer inserted at the thigh joint produces clear yellow juices without any hint of pink. Put all of the quail in 1 pan and cover loosely with aluminum foil to keep the quail warm while you make the sauce.

Discard the fat from the second sauté pan. Add the Curaçao to the pan. Place the pan over medium-high heat and cook for 1 minute. As the liqueur comes to a boil, scrape the bits of caramelized meat juice off the bottom of the pan. Add the cream and grapes and reduce until the cream coats the back of a spoon. Remove the pan from the heat. Add the Cognac and then return the pan to the heat. Bring the cream mixture to a boil, then take the pan off the heat. Swirl in the remaining 3 tablespoons of butter, 1 tablespoon at a time. Season the sauce with salt and pepper.

TO SERVE: Place a mound of wild rice at the top of 6 warmed dinner plates. Lean an apple half against the rice and place 1 teaspoon of currant jelly in each apple half. Remove the thread and twine from each of the quail. Place 2 quail at the bottom of each plate, the legs facing the rice. Dress each plate with ¼ cup of sauce poured over the quail.

Georgia Peach Mousse with Strawberry Coulis

Serves 6

PEACH MOUSSE

1 pound Georgia peaches
2 teaspoons unflavored gelatin
¼ cup water
1 tablespoon lemon juice
2 tablespoons orange juice
1 egg yolk, from a large egg
3 tablespoons sugar
¼ pound white chocolate
2 cups heavy cream

STRAWBERRY COULIS

1 pint strawberries
2 tablespoons lemon juice
2 tablespoons sugar

GARNISH

3 Georgia peaches
1½ cups sugar
24 semisweet chocolate chips
12 mint leaves
2–4 tablespoons confectioners' sugar

MAKING THE MOUSSE: You can use boiling water to remove the skins from peaches as you do with tomatoes. Bring 1½ quarts of water to a boil in a saucepan over high heat. Drop the peaches for the mousse into the water for 30 seconds, then plunge them into ice water to stop the cooking and shrivel the skins. When the peaches have cooled, their skins will slide off easily. Cut the peaches into halves and remove the pits. Chop the peaches coarsely.

Combine the gelatin and water in a small pan. Place the small pan in a larger pan of hot water and allow the gelatin to soften while you finish the peaches.

Purée the peaches with the lemon juice in a food processor. Transfer the purée to a saucepan and simmer it over medium-low heat until it has reduced to ¾ cup (about 30 minutes).

After the peach purée has reduced, remove it from the heat. Add the gelatin and orange juice to the still hot purée, whisking continuously until the gelatin has completely dissolved. Let the purée cool to room temperature.

Beat the egg yolk and sugar in a bowl until the mixture turns a light lemon color.

Melt the white chocolate in the top of a double boiler over simmering water. As soon as it is melted, quickly beat it into the egg yolk. If you allow the white chocolate to cool, it will harden immediately and become very difficult to work with.

Whip the cream until it forms soft peaks.

Fold half the whipped cream and then half the peach purée into the egg yolk-chocolate mixture, then fold in the remaining whipped cream and the rest of the purée. Fill 6 4-ounce molds with the mousse. Refrigerate until ready to serve (at least 4 hours).

MAKING THE COULIS: Hull the strawberries and put them in a food processor with the lemon juice and sugar. Purée until smooth. Taste and add more lemon juice and sugar, as needed. Strain the purée through a fine sieve if you want a seedless *coulis*. You should have 1 cup of sauce.

PREPARING THE PEACH GARNISH: Bring 6 cups of water to a boil in a saucepan over high heat and remove the skins from the 3 peaches, following the above procedure. Cut the skinned peaches into halves and remove the pits.

Bring 4 cups of water and the 1½ cups sugar to a boil in a saucepan over medium-high heat. Cook for 5 minutes. Reduce the heat to medium-low, add the peeled peach halves and simmer for 4–5 minutes or until the peaches are tender but not mushy. Remove them from the poaching liquid. When the peaches have cooled, cut each into 5 or 6 wedges.

TO SERVE: Dip the molds into hot water for 15 seconds, then unmold each serving of mousse onto the center of a dessert plate. Arrange the peach wedges around the mousse. Drizzle 2 tablespoons of coulis down one side of the mousse. Garnish the plate with chocolate chips and mint leaves. Dust each dessert with sifted confectioners' sugar.

The Ritz-Carlton, Atlanta

Atlanta, Georgia

Chilled Asparagus, Fennel and Shrimp

Pumpkin Soup with Saffron in Acorn Squash

*Blue Ridge Mountain Trout with
Braised Spinach and Red Wine Butter Sauce*

Pecan Soufflé with Frangelico Sauce

CHILLED ASPARAGUS, FENNEL AND SHRIMP

Serves 6

SHRIMP

3 cups fish stock (recipe on page 32) or water
⅓ cup celery, diced into ½″ pieces
⅓ cup onions, diced into ½″ pieces
1 bay leaf, crumbled
3 tablespoons lemon juice
1 teaspoon salt
24 large shrimp

36 asparagus spears
2 fennel bulbs

SAUCE

1 pound unsalted butter
2 tablespoons water
¼ cup minced shallots
1 teaspoon white distilled vinegar
½ cup dry white wine
1 bay leaf, whole
½ teaspoon black peppercorns
4 egg yolks, from large eggs
Salt and freshly ground white pepper to taste
Lemon juice to taste

COOKING THE SHRIMP: Bring the fish stock or water, celery, onions, bay leaf, lemon juice and salt to a boil in a large saucepan over high heat. Reduce the heat to medium and simmer for 3 minutes. Add the shrimp. Once the water begins to simmer, cook for another 4 minutes. Drain and cool the shrimp. When cool, peel, devein and chill.

PREPARING THE VEGETABLES: There are several schools of thought on how to prepare asparagus. The traditional method is to bend the stalk gently from tip to stem until it breaks naturally. The stem end is usually tough and fibrous and may be discarded. An alternative is to cut a deep peel off the stem end of the stalk (taking it down 1/16″ all the way around). This eliminates much of the outer fibrous layer and provides a longer portion of edible spear. With either method, you can peel the skin off the entire stalk if you prefer. For appearance's sake, trim all of the spears to the same length, 4″ long.

In a sauté pan large enough to hold the asparagus in one layer (use 2 pans, if necessary, or cook the asparagus in 2 batches), bring 2 inches of salted water to a boil. It's essential to cook the asparagus spears in a shallow pan so they can't bang around and break apart. Boil the asparagus for 3 minutes, or until crisp, but cooked. Immediately plunge them into ice water to stop the cooking.

Remove the 3 largest outside leaves from each fennel bulb. (Use the remainder of the bulbs in another recipe.) Bring a pot of salted water to a boil over high heat. Add the fennel leaves and cook until they're tender, but still firm (5–7 minutes). Plunge them into ice water to stop the cooking.

Drain the vegetables, pat dry and chill.

MAKING THE SAUCE: Clarify the butter by melting it in a small pan over low heat. Skim off the froth of casein that rises to the surface, then spoon out the clear yellow liquid (clarified butter) without disturbing the layer of whey in the bottom of the pan. Set the clarified butter aside.

Bring the water, shallots, vinegar, wine, bay leaf and peppercorns to a boil in a small saucepan over high heat. Lower the heat to medium and cook the mixture until it has reduced by half. Using a fine sieve, strain the mixture into a stainless steel mixing bowl.

For the next step you may either leave the reduction in the stainless steel mixing bowl or transfer it to the top part of a double boiler (as long as it's not aluminum, which can discolor the sauce). In a saucepan or bottom half of a double boiler, bring 2″ of water to a gentle boil over medium heat. Set the mixing bowl or the top part of the double boiler over the water. Add the egg yolks to the reduction. It's important to make sure the water isn't boiling rapidly or the yolks will cook too quickly. Whisk the yolks continuously over the steaming water with a wire whip until they take on a pale, frothy appearance. When the yolks reach this stage, remove the bowl and continue whisking for 2 minutes. This gives the yolks a chance to cool a bit and helps prevent accidental overcooking.

Begin whisking the clarified butter, drop by drop, into the egg yolk mixture. To insure a successful emulsion, add the first drops of butter very slowly. Once the eggs have absorbed about ¼ cup of butter, you can begin adding it in a slow, steady stream, never stopping the whisking. If the sauce seems to be getting too thick, add a teaspoon of warm water. When you've added all the butter, taste the sauce and season with salt, pepper and lemon juice.

TO SERVE: Place 1 fennel leaf, cup-side up, at the top center of each plate. Arrange 6 asparagus spears in the cup of each leaf. Fan 4 shrimp at the bottom of each plate. For each portion, pour about ¼ cup of sauce over the stems of the asparagus so it pools down onto the plate.

GRAND MARNIER SOUFFLÉ
pages 147–48

CHOCOLATE MOUSSE CAKE
pages 151–52

PEAR POACHED IN PORT
page 160

BLUEBERRY MUFFINS
page 161

CARAMEL CUSTARD
page 149

STRAWBERRIES ROMANOFF
page 164

Pumpkin Soup with Saffron in Acorn Squash

Serves 6

3 acorn squashes
2 tablespoons unsalted butter, melted + 6 tablespoons unsalted
    butter
1 pound pumpkin, diced into ¼" pieces
1 small leek
1 cup onions, diced into ¼" pieces
½ cup carrots, diced into ¼" pieces
2 sweet potatoes, peeled and diced into ¼" pieces
5 cups chicken stock (See recipe on page 31.)
½ teaspoon saffron threads, crumbled
1½ cups heavy cream
¼ teaspoon freshly grated nutmeg
Salt and freshly ground white pepper to taste

2 tablespoons finely chopped parsley, for garnish

PREPARING THE ACORN SQUASHES: Preheat oven to 350 degrees.

Cut each acorn squash in half through the stem and scoop out the seeds. Brush the cut edges with melted butter and place them, cut side down, in a roasting pan. Add enough water to the pan to cover the bottom by ⅛". Bake the squashes for 35–45 minutes, or until they're tender but not mushy. Check every 20 minutes to be sure the cut edges are not browning too fast. Add more water, if necessary.

When the squashes have finished baking, allow them to cool. Scoop out enough of the squash flesh on each shell will hold 1 cup of soup, then trim the undersides to sit flat. Use the squash flesh in another recipe.

PREPARING THE SOUP: Steam the diced pumpkin over boiling salted water until just tender (3–4 minutes). Set aside.

To prepare the leek, first cut the green part off the stalk, then cut the leek in half lengthwise to within 1" of the root. Fan the leaves apart as you hold the stalk under running water. Be sure to flush all the sand out. Drain of excess water and dice into ¼" pieces. You should have ½ cup of diced leek.

Melt the remaining butter in a Dutch oven over medium-high heat. Add the leeks, onions, carrots and sweet potatoes. Cook, stirring frequently, for 4–5 minutes. Add twothirds of the pumpkin, all the chicken stock and the saffron. Bring to a boil, lower the heat to medium and simmer for 45 minutes.

Purée the mixture in a food processor, in several batches, until smooth. Strain it through a fine sieve into a clean Dutch oven. Add the remaining pumpkin, the heavy cream and nutmeg. Season with salt and pepper and cook for 5 minutes. If the soup is too thick, add more chicken stock or cream.

TO SERVE: Ladle 1 cup of soup into each of the heated squash shells. Garnish each serving with 1 teaspoon of parsley.

BLUE RIDGE MOUNTAIN TROUT WITH BRAISED SPINACH AND RED WINE BUTTER SAUCE

Serves 6

RED WINE BUTTER SAUCE

1 tablespoon + ½ pound unsalted butter, cut into ½" cubes, chilled
¼ cup minced shallots
¾ cup dry red wine
¾ cup heavy cream
¼ teaspoon white distilled vinegar
⅛ teaspoon cayenne pepper
Salt and freshly ground white pepper to taste
Lemon juice to taste

VEGETABLES AND TROUT

3 tomatoes
3 pounds fresh spinach
6 tablespoons unsalted butter
1 tablespoon dry white wine
1 tablespoon lemon juice
6 whole trout, approximately 8 ounces each, heads and tails removed
Salt and freshly ground black pepper to taste
¼ cup finely chopped shallots

6 lemon wedges, for garnish

MAKING THE SAUCE: Melt the tablespoon of butter in a saucepan over medium-high heat. Add the shallots and cook until translucent (about 3 minutes). Take the pan off the heat and add the red wine. Return the pan to the heat. Bring the wine to a boil, then lower the heat to medium. Let the wine simmer until it has reduced to 2 tablespoons. Be careful not to let it boil away.

Add the heavy cream and reduce the mixture by half. Turn the heat to low and whisk in the ½ pound of butter, 1 cube at a time, emulsifying the butter with the reduction. *Do not boil! If the sauce boils, the emulsion will separate!* The finished consistency should be somewhere between light and heavy cream, a slightly thickened sauce that lightly coats the back of a spoon. Add the vinegar and cayenne, then season with salt, pepper and lemon juice. Strain the sauce through a fine sieve into a saucepan.

Butter sauces will not keep refrigerated. You can, however, hold them for several hours in a warm water bath or in the top part of a double boiler with warm water underneath. Just be sure not to let the water boil.

PREPARING THE VEGETABLES AND COOKING THE TROUT: Bring 6 cups of salted water to a boil. Drop the tomatoes into the water for 15 seconds, then plunge them into ice water to stop the cooking and shrivel the skins. When the tomatoes have cooled their skins will slide off easily. Chop the peeled tomatoes into ½″ pieces, discarding the seeds and stems. Set aside.

To prepare the spinach, grasp each leaf by the stem. Pinch the undersides of the leaf together and pull the stem upward through the leaf. In addition to eliminating the stem, this technique removes the fibrous vein that runs through the leaf. Rinse the leaves thoroughly in cold running water to remove any sand or grit. Shake off excess water.

Bring a large pot with 1″ of salted water to a boil over high heat. Add the spinach, cover the pot and cook until the spinach wilts (about 1 minute). Drain well.

Melt 2 tablespoons of butter in each of 2 large sauté pans over medium heat. Combine the wine and lemon juice. Sprinkle each side of the trout with ½ teaspoon of this mixture and with salt and pepper. Add 3 trout to each pan and cook until they're golden on each side and firm to the touch (6–8 minutes per side).

Using one of the pans, melt 2 tablespoons of the butter over medium-high heat. Add the shallots and cook for 2 minutes. Add the spinach, season with salt and pepper and cook for 2 minutes more.

TO SERVE: Ladle ¼ cup of the red wine butter sauce onto each of 6 warmed dinner plates. Place a mound of spinach in the center of each plate and arrange a trout to one side of it. Garnish with chopped tomato and lemon wedges.

PECAN SOUFFLÉ
WITH FRANGELICO SAUCE

Serves 6

FRANGELICO SAUCE

2 cups light cream
5 egg yolks, from large eggs
2 tablespoons sugar
1 teaspoon vanilla
3 tablespoons Frangelico

SOUFFLÉ

1 tablespoon unsalted butter
1½ cups + 2 tablespoons sugar
2 cups pecans, chopped into ¼″ pieces
4 tablespoons water
2 large eggs
1 egg yolk, from a large egg
½ cup flour
2 cups milk
2–4 tablespoons dark rum
12 egg whites, from large eggs

MAKING THE SAUCE: In a bowl, combine ⅔ cup of the cream with the egg yolks and mix well. Mix the remaining 1⅓ cups of cream with the sugar and vanilla in a saucepan. Cook this mixture over medium heat for 5 minutes. Remove the pan from the heat and slowly add the egg yolk mixture to it. Return the pan to low heat and cook, stirring constantly, until the sauce thickens enough to coat the back of a spoon. *Do not boil or the egg yolks will curdle!* Cooking can take up to 30 minutes. The end result should be a lovely, silky sauce, about the consistency of heavy cream. Add the Frangelico to the sauce and keep it warm while you make the soufflé.

MAKING THE SOUFFLÉ: Preheat oven to 425 degrees.

You can use a 2- or 3-quart soufflé dish for this recipe. If you're using the larger soufflé dish, proceed directly to the next paragraph. If you use the smaller size, you'll have to make a collar so the dish can hold all the soufflé mixture. Figuring the dimensions of the collar is easy. Wrap a piece of string around the outside of the dish to measure its circumference. The collar should be 1⅓ times as long as the string, long enough to wrap around the dish and still overlap. Multiply the height of the dish by 4 to get the width of the collar. Now cut the collar out of foil or parchment paper. Fold the collar in half lengthwise. Rub 1 side with ½ tablespoon of butter. Coat the *inside* of the soufflé dish with ½ tablespoon of butter as well. Wrap the collar around the *outside* of the dish, folded edge up, so that the buttered surface of the collar faces the dish. Tie a piece of string around the middle of the collar to hold it in place. If necessary, secure the collar with a paper clip where its ends overlap at the top. Dust the soufflé dish and the collar with 2 tablespoons of the sugar.

If you use a 3-quart dish, coat it with 1 tablespoon of butter and then dust it with 2 table-spoons of the sugar.

Put the chopped pecans in a roasting pan and roast in the oven for 7–10 minutes. Be careful—they burn easily. Set aside.

Combine ½ cup of the sugar with 2 tablespoons of the water in a heavy-bottomed sauce-pan. Place the pan over medium heat and cook, without stirring, until the sugar has melt-ed and caramelized to a golden brown (about 7 minutes). Remove the pan from the heat and add the remaining 2 tablespoons of water. Taking care not to splatter molten caramel on yourself, stir until the sugar has completely dissolved. Stir in the roasted pecans. Keep the caramelized mixture warm so it doesn't harden while you make the soufflé.

Mix the 2 eggs, the egg yolk, ½ cup of the sugar and the flour together in a cool saucepan to make a paste. Slowly add the milk to the paste, taking care to avoid lumps. Put the pan over medium heat and bring the mixture to a boil, stirring constantly (about 15 min-utes). The mixture should be quite thick. Stir in the caramelized sugar and pecans and add rum to taste. Allow the mixture to cool.

Whip the egg whites until they start to foam. Beat the remaining ½ cup of sugar into the egg whites in a slow, steady stream. Continue until the whites hold stiff (but not dry) peaks. Fold the whites into the cooked mixture. Gently pour the batter into the prepared dish. Bake in the center of the oven until the soufflé puffs above the 3-quart soufflé dish or the collar of the 2-quart soufflé dish (about 25 minutes).

TO SERVE: The soufflé will remain puffed up for only a few minutes, so serve it immediate-ly. Ladle ¼ cup of the Frangelico sauce onto each dessert plate, then top with a generous serving of soufflé.

THE RITZ-CARLTON, LAGUNA NIGUEL

LAGUNA NIGUEL, CALIFORNIA

*Confit of Duck with
Artichoke Bottoms and Oyster Mushrooms*

Anaheim Peppers with Linguini

*Breast of Chicken with Shiitakes and Bok Choy,
Sake-Ginger Sauce*

Nougat Ice Cream

CONFIT OF DUCK WITH ARTICHOKE BOTTOMS AND OYSTER MUSHROOMS

Serves 4

Start this recipe a day and a half in advance, so the duck breasts can marinate for twenty-four hours.

4 small half-breasts of duck, boned, skin on, approximately 4
   ounces each
2 tablespoons kosher salt
2 teaspoons finely chopped fresh thyme (or 1 teaspoon dried)
2–3 cups duck, goose or chicken fat
2 lemons
4 artichokes
1 tablespoon peanut oil
½ cup onions, diced into ¼″ pieces
½ pound oyster mushrooms, sliced ⅛″ thick

VINAIGRETTE

1 tablespoon red wine vinegar
1 minced shallot
3 tablespoons peanut oil
Salt and freshly ground black pepper to taste

¼ pound lamb's lettuce, for garnish
1 bunch enoki mushrooms, for garnish

Place the duck breasts in a stainless steel or glass dish. (Don't use aluminum, as it may interact with the duck breasts.) Sprinkle each breast with ½ tablespoon salt and ½ teaspoon thyme. Cover the dish with plastic wrap and refrigerate overnight.

The next day, scrape any excess salt off the breasts. Set them in a saucepan that will hold them in one layer and add enough fat to cover them by ½″. Put the pan over medium-high heat. As soon as the fat begins to sizzle, turn the heat to medium-low, partially cover the pan and simmer for 2 hours. Remove the breasts from the fat and allow them to cool to room temperature. Discard the fat.

Blend 4 cups of water and the juice of 1 lemon in a mixing bowl. Cut the remaining lemon in half.

Trim the stems from the artichokes and rub the cut spots with a lemon half. Starting at the bottom of each artichoke, remove the leaves by bending them back on themselves. Continue until the remaining leaves begin to form a cone. Turn the artichoke on its side and slice off the cone of leaves just above the top of the heart. Rub the cut spots with a lemon half. Using a paring knife, trim off any remaining dark green leaf bits from the bottom. The artichoke bottom should now be a light green color and nicely rounded. As you finish each artichoke bottom, put it in the bowl with the lemon water.

Heat the tablespoon of peanut oil in a saucepan over medium-high heat. Add the diced onions and sauté until translucent (about 3 minutes). Add the artichoke bottoms and the lemon water to the saucepan and bring it to a boil. Lower the heat to medium and simmer until the artichokes are easily pierced with a knife (20–30 minutes). Remove them from the water and let cool to room temperature. Cut out the chokes (the dense knot of fine, hairlike spines at the heart of the artichoke) and slice the bottoms into pieces ¼″ thick.

MAKING THE VINAIGRETTE: Combine the vinegar and shallots in a small bowl. Whisk in the oil in a slow, steady stream. Season with salt and pepper.

Wash the lamb's lettuce carefully and drain it of excess water. Wrap it in a tea towel and chill the bundle in the refrigerator for 30 minutes.

TO SERVE: Remove the skin from the duck breasts and discard it. Slice the breasts crosswise into medallions ⅓″ thick. Toss the artichokes and oyster mushrooms with the vinaigrette. Divide the artichoke mixture into 4 portions. Mound 1 portion in the center of each of 4 salad plates. Fan the duck medallions around the mixture. Garnish each plate with lamb's lettuce and enoki mushrooms.

ANAHEIM PEPPERS WITH LINGUINI

Serves 4

1 tablespoon peanut oil
4 Anaheim peppers
8 ounces dry linguini
1½ cups heavy cream
2 ounces goat cheese (such as Montrachet)
2 tablespoons unsalted butter
1 tablespoon chives, cut into ⅛″ lengths
Salt and freshly ground black pepper to taste
1 teaspoon minced shallots
2 ounces small or littleneck clams, shucked
2 ounces Louisiana crayfish tails, peeled

Heat the peanut oil in a small sauté pan over very high heat. Add the peppers and cook, turning often, until the skins blacken and blister, but not so long that the meat of the peppers begins to soften (about 30 seconds). Place the peppers in a paper bag. The peppers' residual heat will steam the skins loose. After 5 minutes, remove them from the bag. The skins should slip off easily. Slit each pepper in half lengthwise, leaving the halved stems attached, and remove the seeds. Rinse the pepper halves under cold water to eliminate any remaining skin or seeds. Set aside.

Bring a large pot of salted water to a boil. Add the linguini, stirring rapidly until the water returns to a boil. Boil the pasta for 9 minutes, then tip it into a colander and immediately rinse with cold water to stop the cooking. Set aside.

Bring 1 cup of the cream to a boil in a saucepan over high heat. Reduce the heat to medium and simmer until it has reduced to ½ cup. Season with salt and pepper. Remove the pan from the heat and cover to keep warm.

Whisk the remaining ½ cup of the cream with the cheese in a small saucepan. Reduce the mixture over medium heat until it coats the back of a spoon. Stir in 1 tablespoon of the butter and the chives. Season with salt and pepper. Set aside.

Melt the remaining tablespoon of butter in a sauté pan over medium-high heat. Add the shallots and cook for 3 minutes. Add the clams and crayfish and cook an additional 3 minutes. Season with salt and pepper.

Stuff each pepper with about 2 tablespoons of the seafood mixture.

Ten minutes before serving, preheat the oven to 450 degrees. Heat the peppers thoroughly in the oven (about 5 minutes). Warm the cream-cheese mixture in a large sauté pan over medium heat. Add the linguini and toss until heated all the way through.

TO SERVE: Mound the pasta in 4 warmed soup bowls. Arrange the stuffed peppers atop the pasta. Drizzle 1 tablespoon of reduced cream over the seafood mixture in each pepper half.

Breast of Chicken with Shiitakes and Bok Choy, Sake-Ginger Sauce

Serves 4

4 baby bok choy, each about 3″ long (or 1 head mature bok choy)
½ cup water
1 teaspoon salt
3 tablespoons unsalted butter
1 pound shiitake mushrooms, sliced ¼″ thick
Salt and freshly ground black pepper to taste
4 large half-breasts of chicken, boned and skinned, approximately 7
   ounces each

SAKE-GINGER SAUCE

1 cup water
2 tablespoons fresh ginger, diced into ⅛″ pieces
½ cup veal stock (See recipe on page 30.)
1 cup chicken stock (See recipe on page 31.)
½ cup sake
2 tablespoons unsalted butter
Salt and freshly ground pepper to taste

GARNISH

2 cups chicken stock (See recipe on page 31.)
4 ounces transparent noodles (available at Oriental markets)
¼ cup scallions, sliced on the bias into ¼″ pieces

If you're fortunate enough to have procured baby bok choy, rinse each head without breaking the leaves off the core, shake off the excess water and proceed directly to the next paragraph. If you're using a single head of mature bok choy, separate the leaves from the core and wash them well. You should have 12–16 leaves. Trim off all but 1″ of the white stem.

Bring the water, the salt and 2 tablespoons of the butter to a boil in a large sauté pan over high heat. Add the bok choy and cover. Reduce the heat to low and simmer until tender (10–15 minutes). Lift the lid every 5 minutes or so to give the bok choy a stir. Remove the bok choy from the pan and drain well. Leave the cooking liquid in the sauté pan—you will use it again. Allow the bok choy to cool.

Melt the remaining tablespoon of butter in a sauté pan over medium-high heat. Add the shiitake mushrooms and cook, stirring frequently, until tender (about 5 minutes). Season with salt and pepper and allow to cool.

Place each chicken breast between 2 sheets of plastic wrap, skin-side (the round side) down. Pound them with a heavy-bottomed saucepan or flat meat tenderizer to even out the thickness of the breasts and break down some of the muscle fibers. Be careful not to tear the flesh.

To roll the flattened chicken breasts around the vegetables, begin by seasoning the bone side (the flat side) of the breasts with salt and pepper. Divide the bok choy and mushrooms into 4 equal portions. Lay the bok choy leaves over the seasoned side of the breasts and mound the mushrooms down the center. If you're using baby bok choy, lay 1 head on the seasoned side of each breast, molding the mushroom mixture around the cabbage. Roll each breast into a sausage shape.

Roll each breast in plastic wrap. Each breast should be encased in 2 or 3 layers of wrap, with about 4″ of wrap left on either end. Twist the ends closed and tie them with twine. The breasts should be wrapped securely, but not so tightly that steam escaping during the cooking will burst the packages. When the wrapping is completed, each breast should resemble a large party favor.

Place the chicken rolls in the sauté pan with the bok choy cooking liquid. If necessary, add enough water so there's ½″ liquid in the pan (after adding the chicken). Cover the pan, place it over medium heat and simmer until a thin skewer penetrates the chicken without resistance (about 20 minutes). Turn the chicken rolls at least 3 times so they cook evenly. Remove the chicken rolls from the liquid and allow them to rest 5 minutes before unwrapping.

MAKING THE SAUCE: Bring 1 cup of water to a boil in a small pot. Add the ginger and cook for 1 minute.

After cooking, strain the ginger and discard the water. Place the ginger in a clean saucepan and add the veal and chicken stocks. Bring everything to a boil over high heat, then lower the heat to medium. Reduce the mixture until only ¼ cup of liquid remains. Add the sake and simmer for 2 minutes. Take the pan off the heat and whisk in the butter, 1 tablespoon at a time. Season with salt and pepper.

PREPARING THE NOODLE GARNISH: Bring the remaining 2 cups of chicken stock to a boil in a saucepan over high heat. As soon as the stock boils, remove the pan from heat. Soak the noodles in the stock for 5 minutes, then drain and divide into 4 portions.

TO SERVE: Carefully remove the chicken breasts from the plastic. Slice each breast into medallions ¾″ thick. Place one portion of the noodles in the center of each of 4 warmed plates. Arrange the chicken in a circle of overlapping medallions around the noodles. Sprinkle chopped scallions over the noodles and dress each portion of chicken with 3 tablespoons of sauce.

NOUGAT ICE CREAM

Serves 4

1 cup + 12 blanched almonds, whole
1 tablespoon unsalted butter, softened
¼ cup water
½ cup sugar
½ cup honey
8 egg whites, from large eggs
1¼ cups *crème anglaise* (See recipe on page 148.)
2 cups heavy cream

8 mint leaves, for garnish

Preheat oven to 350 degrees.

Place the almonds in a pan and roast them until they're golden (6–10 minutes). Set 12 of the almonds aside for a garnish. The rest will be used to make the nougat.

Coat a baking sheet with the butter.

Combine the sugar and water in a heavy-bottomed saucepan. Place the pan over medium heat and cook, without stirring, until all the sugar has melted into a golden caramel (about 7 minutes). Add all but 12 of the almonds and remove the pan from the heat. Pour the mixture onto the prepared baking sheet and allow it to cool.

Heat the honey in a heavy-bottomed saucepan until it registers 248 degrees on a candy thermometer. Whip the egg whites until they hold firm (but not dry) peaks. While continuing to whip the egg whites, add the honey in a steady stream to make a meringue. Keep beating until the meringue cools to room temperature. When the sugar-almond mixture (nougat) has solidified, break it up and put it into a food processor. Process until the nougat is finely chopped, but not a powder. Remove all but 2 tablespoons of the nougat and fold it into the meringue.

Process the remaining nougat into a powder. Stir it into the crème anglaise and set aside.

Whip the cream until it holds soft peaks. Fold it into the meringue. Put the nougat mixture into a 2-quart rectangular mold, cover it with plastic wrap and place it in the freezer. Allow it to freeze 4 hours before unmolding.

TO SERVE: Place the mold in hot water for 15 seconds. Turn it out onto a serving platter. Garnish with the toasted almonds and mint leaves. Slice the ice cream into ½" portions and serve with nougat crème anglaise.

INDEX